81 LESSONS FROM THE SKY

GENERAL AVIATION

FLETCHER MCKENZIE

SSP

81 LESSONS FROM THE SKY

NEAR MISSES AND STORIES FROM
81 GENERAL AVIATION PILOTS
IN AUSTRALIA, USA AND THE UNITED KINGDOM

This edition published 2021 by Squabbling Sparrows Press

ISBN 978-0-4734199-43 (Paperback edition)
ISBN 978-0-4734199-67 (Ebook edition)

Published by Squabbling Sparrows Press
PO Box 4213, Marewa, Napier 4143
New Zealand

ALSO BY FLETCHER MCKENZIE

This book is dedicated to all the aviators who made the time to record their stories contained within these pages.

And to the aviators who came before me - whose lessons help me fly safely - I really do thank you.

This book is also for my Dad, who passed on his passion for aviation.

And for my wife, my mother, my brother, and my girls - Sasha and Jetta, who have trusted me with their lives and who have enjoyed flying with me for many, many years.

"Everything we know in aviation, every rule in the rule book, every procedure we have, we know because someone somewhere died…. We have purchased at great cost, lessons literally bought with blood that we have to preserve as institutional knowledge and pass on to succeeding generations. We cannot have the moral failure of forgetting these lessons and then having to relearn them."

Chesley Sullenberger

CONTENTS

FOREWORD

SCOTT MCKENZIE

It's getting harder to invent new ways of killing yourself in aviation. Some unfortunate individual has, most likely, already done it. We are lucky in aviation, there is a culture of analysing incidents and accidents to find out what happened and putting processes in place to prevent it happening again.

Our early pioneers gave us the gift of a safety culture that is well ahead of other industries. It is not perfect but better than most. It is great to learn from your mistakes. Eleanor Roosevelt said, *"It is better to learn from other people's mistakes. You can't live long enough to make them all yourself."*

I grew up around aviation, my parents still own an aviation business. For a long time I accepted that pilots dying was just a by-product of aviation. It was a regular occurrence that one of my parents' friends or acquaintances would crash. Then it started happening to my friends. It feels indiscriminate. Some people would make mistakes and nothing would happen. For others, the cruel hand of fate would deal the harshest blow at the first misstep. Everyone should return home to their family at the end of the day. On many occasions it comes down to our own vigilance, decision making and actions that keep us, or others, safe.

I watched a documentary on Bob Hoover, a gentleman blessed with great skills and humility. There were several well-known pilots on the documentary who said that they owed their lives to Bob. They listened to his experiences at one of his seminars and, when they had an emergency a few years later, the Bob Hoover file came from the depths of their memory and helped them deal with the emergency. That is what this book is about, an opportunity to learn from other people's mistakes and apply them to ensure you successfully return home at the end of the day.

I first met Fletcher McKenzie when I was flying in the RNZAF Formation Aerobatic Team. No relation, but a brother from another mother. He was filming for his show FlightPathTV. Whenever I could help out I did, including attaching a camera to the T-tail of my father's MD500D for a display at the Ohakea Airshow. We lament to this day that the camera didn't work, because it was a great display and would have been an amazing perspective.

Fletcher is also heavily involved with the Entrepreneur's Organisation (EO). At an airshow in 2009 we arranged a Red Checker's/EO/Yak Team hospitality tent on the flight line. An epic airshow with a great bunch of people. It is the people that make those events, and I love the people involved with aviation. Fletcher is enthusiastic about aviation and sharing stories about people and aircraft.

One of the key tenets for EO is learning from other people's mistakes. Learning from the mistakes of others accelerates success. Taking that philosophy to his flying, Fletcher has gathered articles and reports to accelerate his learning and success in aviation. I commend him for bringing these together in a book that should be on the coffee table in every flight school and aero club.

One day, one of the lessons in this book might be that file that pops up from the depths of your memory to save your life. That moment of doubt which prompts you to recheck the oil cap or rudder lock, check the fuel cock position, or query a radio call.

If there is any doubt, there is no doubt. Listen to that doubt, trust your gut, take action. And, if you almost invent a new way of killing yourself, have the courage to write it down so you can accelerate other people's success in this fantastic profession that is aviation.

Scott McKenzie
Scott McKenzie served 22 years with the Royal New Zealand Air Force, including four operational deployments, and four seasons in the formation aerobatic team (two as leader). A Category (H) & (A) instructor, he retired as a Wing Commander in 2017. He conducted utility longline operations in New Zealand and Canada on power-line, drilling and conservation work and is now an aviation consultant.

www.pappus.co.nz

INTRODUCTION

MATT HALL

I was quite young when I started my aviation career.

At 14-years-of-age I started my formal training in a glider, though I had been flying for many years prior to that with my dad. I put a lot of effort in and was fortunate enough that not much went wrong in my young and inexperienced years. I say this is good fortune, as I was probably not armed very well at the time if things did go wrong.

When I graduated from RAAF pilot training with my wings, I was pulled aside by a number of instructors who gave me a bit of a chest poking... *"of all the pilots I know, you are the one most likely to kill yourself"* was the gist of what they were saying. This was due to the fact I had done reasonably well on pilot course, and was probably starting to believe that I could handle anything in a plane. Once again, I listened, and took it in, though deep down I don't think I felt anything could really happen to me.

Then things started happening to me...

I had engine fires. I had engine failures. I had a near miss with the ground. I had a near miss with another aircraft. I had missiles shot at me. I had friends die. I crashed a plane...

Over the years I have started to have more and more appreciation of the risks in aviation. While it is such a fabulous career and hobby, it is also unforgiving and deadly. The old saying that *'there are old pilots, and bold pilots, but no old and bold pilots'* is very true.

It led me to understand how to be a successful fighter pilot. I looked not only at staying alive inside of aviation, but also how to be the best pilot I could be. People would ask me if fighter pilots are arrogant. I would respond that good fighter pilots are confident, not arrogant. When asked for the difference, I would answer that confident pilots believe they can do anything within their and the aircraft limits, though are still willing to listen to advice. Arrogant pilots have the same belief, though don't listen.

So, I have been listening all my career, not only to be the best I could possibly be, but also as safe as possible. If you want to be a safer, and a better pilot, learning from other people's misfortunes is a must. And this is what this book is about. It allows people to 'listen' to other people's stories, other people who have had misfortune though are prepared to talk about it. Hopefully this will also encourage you to share your own stories, and be prepared to 'admit' when you have made a mistake. It will not only help you learn from your own mistakes, but you may just save someone else's life.

Enjoy the read.

Matt Hall

A third-generation pilot, a decorated former RAAF Fighter Combat Instructor, international unlimited aerobatic competitor, Red Bull Air Race World Championships pilot and airfield owner.

www.matthallracing.com

PREFACE
FLETCHER MCKENZIE

"The air is an extremely dangerous, jealous and exacting mistress. Once under the spell most lovers are faithful to the end, which is not always old age. Even those masters and princes of aerial fighting, the survivors of fifty mortal duels in the high air who have come scatheless through the War and all its perils, have returned again and again to their love and perished too often in some ordinary commonplace flight undertaken for pure amusement."

Sir Winston Churchill KG OM CH TD DL FRS RA

'In The Air,' Thoughts and Adventures, 1932.

My father passed his passion for aviation on to me. He was a man who loved reading, learning, and talking about aircraft. Before he died, he was following the developments on the 787 and the progress of the A380, and we had many discussions around the classic argument of who is better - Boeing or Airbus.

In his early years, my father worked for the National Airways Corporation (NAC). Whenever we drove to Tauranga or past the Kaimai Ranges to Matamata, he would talk about the DC-3 that crashed into the Kaimai Ranges in 1963 and how he'd known one of the flight attendants onboard. I still have the DC-3 model he made for his office, hand-painted in the NAC colours. I'd pulled it apart as a child but its battered remains live on in my own office. I always wondered how and why that DC-3 had crashed in 1963, and it wasn't until years later when I read Rev. Dr Richard Waugh's book on the accident, that I knew what had happened.

As a teenager in the Air Training Corps, I was selected for a gliding camp at RNZAF Base Hobsonville, where I learnt the theory of flight, going solo at the age of 16. The youngest instructor on that course was 37, and had a number of flying awards to his name. Some months after that course, he was killed in a glider crash. To a teenage boy, it was impossible to understand how that could happen to an experienced pilot.

In 1990, one of the requirements of my Bursary Maths paper was to complete a statistical project. I chose a subject I was interested in - aviation, specifically *Aircraft Accidents 1979 to 1989*. I had to find the relevant statistical information and build out theories explaining what the numbers suggested. I have constantly referred back to those findings as accidents occurred in the aviation industry, to see if my teenage hypothesis was correct, given the circumstances of the given incident. The correlation has always been interesting.

Safety was paramount when I flew gliders as an Air Training Corps cadet, but it wasn't until I began my Private Pilot Licence (PPL) training, that I began to understand the factors which would lead to an accident. *Human Factors* was the most interesting book I had read for years. The deeper I read into the situations pilots got into, the more I understood the factors which can lead to poor decision making.

In 2010, I began production of the television show *FlightPathTV* - a magazine style television show on aviation. *FlightPathTV* was on air in sixty-one countries (including the Discovery Channel with Rugby All Black Captain Richie McCaw), and has been translated into various languages including Mandarin.

Over a period of eighteen months, we interviewed nearly one hundred pilots from around the world. I spent hours listening to personal stories from pilots on what inspired them and how they become pilots. The first time I heard that one of our interviewed pilots had been killed in an aviation accident crushed me. The pilots we interviewed were incredibly experienced, and the news of his death was inconceivable. Over the last seven years, this toll has risen to six pilots, with even more involved in non-critical accidents. Why is this number so high?

As part of my ongoing role in filming aviation stories, I meet and interview experienced pilots from around the world to find out what they read and what inspires them to be safer pilots. What did they do? How did they do it? And how have they changed their processes to become safer in the air?

Being a private pilot and having a young family, I read every aviation safety magazine and numerous books on flying to learn from those incidents - especially the near miss stories, to ensure I don't make the same mistakes. Through other pilots sharing their stories, I become a safer pilot.

I work with a number of entrepreneurs from around the world, through EO (Entrepreneurs Organisation), leading them in strategy planning and training them to experience share between each other and to learn from mistakes - the good and the bad. This is a proven process I want to add to in the aviation community.

EO is a global, peer-to-peer network of more than 13,000 influential business owners in 52 countries, and they employ a unique communication model which provides unparalleled access to the wisdom of your peers during confidential monthly meetings. It is called 'Forum'.

Forum came out of the desire to have a safe environment to share and learn from others' experiences. Extensive research was undertaken to develop the concept. Building from early small group theory, the key objective was to create a supportive environment for members without fear of confidentiality being broken, and without risk of being judged by others, to share, learn and grow within a close group of peers. The language protocol supports the risk being taken by others in Forum, and is what makes Forum a safe place. The "Speak only from Experience" Gestalt Mindset encourages people to find their own answers.

Every time I've sat in a cockpit, and especially since I started flying different aircraft and attaining different ratings, I think back to my sixteen-year-old self learning to fly a Blanik L-13 glider and grappling with understanding how the aircraft performed - I didn't even have my drivers licence at that stage, and here I was up in the air.

From there, I fast forward to understanding the flight characteristics and feeling of the stall buffet of the Cessna 172 when doing a streamer cut in the fastest possible time at the New Zealand Flying Nationals. And onto realising how fast I had to react if we lost power on a twin engined aircraft upon landing or taking off and how quickly we needed to react because of the asymmetric effect.

Mental alertness and knowing what the correct reaction will be before something happens while towing a glider are essential. The ongoing constant monitoring and recognising, at low levels, the glider behind me and if it was going to get out of position before it was too late to pull the tow line.

To then flying an aerobatic sequence in the "1000 metre box" at my first aerobatic competition without a safety pilot. Understanding how and what the aircraft was doing or sometimes not doing because of my input, coupled with knowing exactly where I was in terms of space and ground reference and keeping a close eye on my altimeter for height below and above.

One of my most exciting moments was being taught how to land and take off on the water in a Beaver float plane. Taxiing on the ground and on the sea was interesting - similar strange sensations and learnings, a little bit like turning a Yak-52, so different but yet once you get it, it is effective.

It has been a journey of learning with so many different pilot types mixed in - a constant number of lessons from the sky, but more importantly, realising that the reflection and time taken afterwards is where the learning starts. A number of my non-aviation friends think I am crazy. In reality, I am just overly passionate about aviation. The feeling of freedom is incredible and I couldn't get the same excitement and adrenaline anywhere else.

Remember that Bursary Maths assignment back in 1990? I was studying Math With Statistics, Maths With Calculus, and Physics so I could join the Royal New Zealand Air Force. Which was why choosing aviation as my subject matter was so easy. As I researched aircraft accidents in New Zealand, without the benefit of the internet, I was forced to pick up the phone to call the office of the New Zealand Civil Aviation Authority (CAA). From that phone call, I discovered I could purchase journals covering all the aviation accidents in New Zealand. I bought eleven of those journals.

Suddenly I was reading about aircraft incidents, and at times fatal crashes. As a teenager, it had an effect on me. The assignment was completed, and there were some interesting results. But now that I am part of the aviation industry, the numbers are more than just statistics published in a journal. They are someone's life tragically cut short, someone's mother or father, a son or a daughter. That is the hard part of statistics - when they are numbers on a page there is just no emotion involved.

I had planned to republish that research paper, and incorporate the latest statistics, but I was not 100% sure how the report and its findings would help the industry. Whilst thinking about publishing, and the desired outcome, I started writing a few stories myself, the first one after a personal air incident. I was encouraged by Adam Eltham, a good friend and instructor, to write about that incident, to understand the learnings from the event. And that is how this book began.

Fletcher McKenzie

PROLOGUE

"Most accidents originate in actions committed by reasonable, rational individuals who were acting to achieve an assigned task in what they perceived to be a responsible and professional manner."

Peter Harle
Director of Accident Prevention
Transportation Safety Board of Canada
(And former RCAF pilot)

THE BIG BLUE SKY, the heavens above. Scattered with clouds big and small, adorned with rainbows, and dappled with sunlight. Through the ages, children, adults, dreamers and designers, leaders, marauders and tyrants have looked to the sky above and wondered how to get there. For me, the sky is a place I'm often in, either as a passenger in a commercial airliner, or in a smaller aircraft I am flying.

I love the freedom flying provides - to move in a multi axis dimension, going where you want, when you want - as free as a bird.

Total freedom... although physics has a part to play here. With freedom comes risk. And I ask you, is the risk worth the reward?

Freedom is worth the risk. And I know the risks. Sadly, many people have faced those risks and have not survived.

The aviation industry helps economies grow by expanding markets and allowing investors, and tourists, to spread their capital further. However, with any reward, risk is close behind. From when the Wright Brothers first flew over the Kittyhawk plains in 1903, more than 153,624 people have been killed in aviation accidents (ACRO statistics). Not too bad considering that 4.1 billion people moved commercially around the globe in 2017 (ICAO statistics).

Since the Montgolfier brothers launched a balloon on a tether with Jean-François Pilâtre de Rozier in 1783, people have been able to soar with the birds. And men and woman have learned lessons from their experiences in the skies. Those lessons have been documented and passed on to future aviators - some religiously, some not so much.

As a pilot I do certain things and operate a certain way so that I don't become another statistic. However, in those first few years I didn't understand the importance of the lessons (or procedures) put in place to ultimately save my life. Those lessons and practices have now become a way of life for me and have spread into other areas in my life - my life practices and my daily habits.

One lesson is from the book *Black Box Thinking* by Matthew Syed. The author talks about the United States Army Air Forces calling in psychologist Alphonse Chapanis to investigate instances of pilots making dangerous and unexplainable errors after landing safely. Pilots landing a B-17 bomber (made by Boeing) would safely touch down and then mistakenly retract the landing gear, where the obvious would happen - the B-17 bomber would scrape along the ground, exploding into sparks and flames. Mr Chapanis interviewed pilots but also studied the cockpits of the aircraft. He found that on the B-17 bombers, the levers controlling the landing gear and flaps not only looked identical but were situated next to each other. A pilot would lower the landing gear and then, after landing, would raise the flaps. Maybe due to fatigue, the pilot could mistakenly grab the wrong lever and retract the landing gear when he meant to raise the flaps. The solution? The designers attached a small wheel to the landing gear control and a flap-shaped wedge to the flap control - so they looked exactly like the actual item they were controlling. Pilots could feel which lever was the correct lever, thereby eliminating this problem of accidentally raising the landing gear after landing safely.

I always wondered why, in the Cessna 152, there is a straight lever knob used to select flap. I have piloted a Piper Aztec and a Tecnam P2008, both with retractable landing gear, and both have a lever with a wheel/tyre on it. It wasn't until reading Black Box Thinking that I knew it came from a 1940s ergonomic design decision.

We learn from the mistakes of others.

One story I've included highlights this case - **Reading On A Train Saved My Life**. The pilot explains that the reason for his survival was due to a book he'd read on a train years before, about sensory problems at night, where fighter pilots in World War II were mysteriously crashing after night take-offs. Given the chain of events which could have led to a fatal accident, luckily the last link in the chain was broken thanks to a book on a train, which allowed the modern day pilot to recognise the symptoms and make the correct inputs.

The Learning that started it all...

Chapter 2 covers Complacency & Fatigue, and in the story ACCIDENT REPORT, the pilot talks about the simple mistake of thinking that they were landing on the runway but in fact it was rough ground. They walked away from the landing but the aircraft required extensive repair work to become airworthy again. The pilot stated, "*My brain had locked into a decision and my concentration was on the technicalities of making another smooth landing.*"

Their story reminded me of a similar incident I experienced in 2009 - my mind took over and even though it was confused, it wanted to say that we were exactly where we should have been, even though this was far from the truth.

We had flown down to the Classic Fighters Airshow in Omaka, at the top of the South Island of New Zealand. It is one of the best airshows I have been to in the world and I've been to quite a few. It is perfect for filming with the golden hills as a stunning backdrop. The airshow usually features Sir Peter Jackson's squadrons of WWI aircraft, and a myriad of WWII aircraft.

We were filming the airshow as part of our television show *FlightPathTV*, and had flown the Cessna 172 down with all our camera equipment – a 3.5 hour trip. For the trip home, the weather looked clear, not a cloud in the sky. I had a chat with some other pilots who said *if it looks good, go straight up the middle of the island.* It's a beautiful scenic route in good weather. Those pilots went onto say that I would need to contact Ohakea to transit through the control zone. So we did.

After take off, we dashed across the Cook Straight crossing along with a few other aircraft coming back from the airshow. Passing Paraparaumu we said our goodbyes via wing wagging and a radio call as they went on to land at Fox Pine airfield. We carried on. Soon we entered the Ohakea control zone and I radioed to ask what the weather was like up ahead. Ohakea replied that it was pretty much clear. To this day I believed them, and I believed that from their point of view it was in fact clear. However to us in the Cessna 172 it was very much not clear - the cloud had become thicker and lower, and the valleys higher – this is when the sphincter test started to kick in. I was getting alarmed. Then the turbulence started to really upset our day. Trying to get a fix on the direction we were flying was near impossible – the compass was swinging wildly and the ADF was a waste of space - moving out of sync every few minutes.

I radioed Ohakea to get a position report, which did not help as I had no correlation to what they said versus what I could see on the map. In hindsight, I should have asked for the map coordinates. Soon we were out of radio range and were on our own. As we spied pockets of clear space we'd head towards it. I remember pressing on regardless. How lost could we get? I guessed we'd be able to find a reference point as to where we were, at some stage.

As I write this, it sounds like the most idiotic thing to do. A recipe for disaster. But when you are in the moment you push on – we had full tanks when we left, so that was one plus in our favour.

We broke out of the darkness above a massive ridge and saw the sun peaking through through the clouds, and I recall saying to my copilot, "*Lets head over there.*" And that is where we headed - to the fair weather and it was so clear it felt like heaven. As we got closer, we were able to see a number of reference points, including a large lake. I said to my copilot, "*Wow, Lake Taupo looks big!*" As we looked at the reference points, we tried to relate them back to the map and make them fit. Our view had a mountain, water, the outcrops, we were definitely at the southern end of Lake Taupo - New Zealand's largest lake. Or that is what we thought. It was confusing that houses and buildings were on the map, but weren't on the piece of land we were looking at. My mind even wondered how they managed to demolish the buildings so fast and have vegetation regrow so quickly...

As we got closer to the water, I was amazed how large Lake Taupo was - we couldn't see the northern end. Lake Taupo was formed by the world's largest volcanic eruption 70,000 years ago, so my mind had strayed to pondering on how that must have been a big eruption. Then, the pieces of evidence began falling into place, and the thoughts inside my mind dissolved, and alarms started going off in my head. I looked closer at the map for other areas of water. We discussed that we did turn to the right a lot, but surely we hadn't turn that far, 90 degrees – as opposed to travelling north? But we had.

This incident that made me feel foolish and I am still shocked to see how human factors and assumption nearly caused an accident. Only the full fuel tanks were on our side that day.

On returning to my aviation club I telephoned a friend, and a B Cat instructor, to discuss how to ensure I learnt from this incident. They told me to write it down. So I wrote out what happened, to learn from my mistakes. It is replicated unedited below for you:

Napier Incident 13 April 2009

We planned to fly up the coast with another aircraft. We were headed to Pauanui and after talking with other experienced pilots, they suggested to go up through the Desert Road as it should be great weather and easy to navigate.

All weather reports indicated good weather, however on the morning it seemed that there was some cloud around the Wellington Region and Straits.

I did a route plan and saw that we could ask to go through Ohakea airspace and through the Valley in case of low cloud. I assumed we would be able

I was using a 1:250,000 chart and the area was on the edge of the chart.

I asked Ohakea control for clearance through the zone – cleared to 1500. As we went past Ohakea and overhead bulls we tracked left and turned left even more to avoid rain and showers ahead. My position I assumed was heading North West, this was hard to work out due to turbulence and wind moving the aircraft around. The DI was constantly out of position, as we noticed on the fight down previously. We were also in low cloud and low height we became disorientated on our direction and position. OC cleared us to 1500, then had to climb to 2000 due to terrain.

Ohakea Control advised me I was clear of the zone. It was at this point that I was trying to see where we were, I asked and said we assume we are close to Marton. OC said *yes, approx. a few miles* is what I thought he said. At a low height it was hard to work out where we were. The road, train tracks and cliffs I assumed were in position A, but now looking at the map we were possible at position B.

I did radio OC to see if we were busting airspace due to terrain, there was no reply. We did encounter turbulence and severe down draughts – I was working hard to maintain comfortable flight.

We saw some sunlight in a valley and decided to aim for it to get out of the cloud. Upon getting over the mountain we saw the water, what we thought was Lake Taupo. It was clear and sunny, and looking at the map it made sense, we were over Turangi. I remember the finger of land - but my mind was confused, but I was sure we were where we were. I made a radio call stating my position.

Then the radio call came, it was Napier Tower, as the radio call happened I realised what had happened - we were over Napier and possibly in the Napier control zone - I made a hard turn and answered the radio call, I explained how we had become lost. We ended up at Napier not our intended route of Turangi, ATC gave us a compass heading towards Taupo which we followed and refuelled and carried onto Pauanui with no further issue.

Why did it happen? What steps should I take to ensure it will not happen again?

This was in the days before I had any type of GPS system. Now I wouldn't fly without GPS, and my Spidertracks tracking system. They add another layer of complexity - technology, which is covered in Chapter 8 - Technology & Automation. Now I always plan first and map plot and then use my GPS as a back up, ensuring I am correct with my map reading.

I really like cheese - Gorgonzola and Emmental are my favourites. Emmental has walnut-sized holes and is considered to be one of the most difficult cheeses to be produced because of its complicated hole-forming fermentation process. Delicious with a glass of wine.

Why am I talking about cheese? The concept of the "Swiss

Cheese Model" is about accident causation. It is a model used in risk analysis and risk management, including aviation safety, engineering, healthcare, emergency service organisations, and as the principle behind layered security (also in computing). The Swiss Cheese Model of accident causation illustrates that, although there are many layers of defence between hazards and accidents, there are flaws in each layer that, if aligned, can allow the accident to occur.

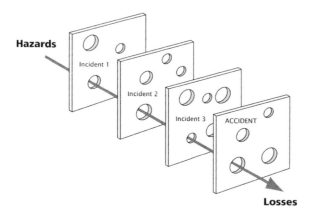

I love the analogy of the Swiss Cheese Model. An organisation's defences against failure are modelled as a series of barriers, represented as slices of cheese, stacked side by side, in which the risk of a threat becoming a reality is mitigated by the differing layers and types of defences which are "layered" behind each other. The holes in the slices represent weaknesses in individual parts of the system and are continually varying in size and position across the slices. The system produces failures when a hole in each slice momentarily aligns, permitting (in Reason's words) *"a trajectory of accident opportunity"*, so that a hazard passes through holes in all of the slices, leading to a failure or accident. Therefore, in theory, lapses and weaknesses in one defence do not allow a risk to materialise, since other defences also exist, to prevent a single point of failure. The model was originally formally propounded by Dante Orlandella and

James T. Reason of the University of Manchester [1] and has gained widespread acceptance.

If I take the model (see diagram below) and use it in the case of our flight getting lost and roaming into Napier airspace, we were lucky that we did indeed hit Napier airspace, if we hadn't we would've been really lost and only had so much fuel in our tanks before we would have had to land somewhere, and not necessarily somewhere good.

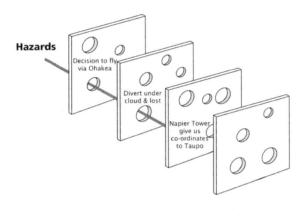

Adapted from the Swiss cheese model of accident causation. Created: 18 March 2014. Creative Commons - *Davidmack*

Footnote: 1 - Reason 1990

I wanted to show how powerful these stories have been for me; how many of these stories made me think about how I would approach that same situation the pilot was confronted with. My story is just one of the many stories that made me think further about what I need to do to mitigate risk before or during my flying operations.

Some years ago I read a story in Vector magazine published by the New Zealand Civil Aviation Authority (CAA) about a seat incident with a Cessna. The incident occurred after the pilot pulled back the control column upon take off, the aircraft seat then let go and the pilot holding onto the control column pulled back as the seat slid backwards, the aircraft lurched up into the stall. Luckily they were able to gain control and the aircraft landed safely without further incident. The chair rail locking device had failed. I remember reading and thinking, god I hope that doesn't happen to me. Interestingly though I never looked at the seat structure or asked any questions or talked to anyone or checked to see if any modifications had been completed on the 172 I usually fly.

Simply after reading that article, during my preflight checks, I always gave the seat a good shake to ensure it is steady and that the locking mechanism worked, and once I was in the aircraft and buckled in I always shook the hell out of the chair to ensure it will not move on take off. But I never closely examined the chair locking system or tried to understand the structure of the seat in the 172. I *assumed* that the club, the owners and our maintenance engineer would have looked at this... Was I right to assume this?

Reading the story "SEAT FAILURE ON TAKE-OFF" in Chapter 1, got me wondering just exactly how the chair legs in the Cessna are locked in place. I'd assumed that all four legs were locked in. So I decided the next time I was out at the club I would investigate further. Upon closer inspection, I looked at the back legs and there were none, *okay* I thought, there must be two at the front. To my amazement no, just one leg on the inside was used to lock the chair. A one 5mm diameter steel rod was holding my 90kg frame into place.

I recently flew a passenger who was 110kg. When the Cessna was designed in the 1960s, the average pilot was around 65-75kgs, so potentially one locked leg was all that was required. But I couldn't believe that I never realised there was only one locked leg - I was shocked. I discussed this with a friend who suggested I should design and manufacture a locking device. So I googled seat locking devices for Cessna to see what was on the market and wow, there were a few.

Mostly designed for the Cessna taildraggers and the issue they were having. I only recently found out that there is a locking device on the market for a Cessna 172.

I have since bought that locking device for my seat, to ensure that it is one less hole in "Swiss cheese slice" that I don't need to worry about. It locks onto the rails and it only acts as a stopper if the seats moves back.

I hope that when you read these stories, you are able to make notes and look at removing a few holes from the layers (of cheese) in your flying, and build up new habits to ensure that your flying will be even safer than it is now.

But still, the best investment I've ever made in my flying career was a $1 exercise book from the supermarket. With a simple pen or pencil I can make notes, jot down thoughts, and any learnings from every single flight.

As a student pilot, I would read all the stories in the Vector magazine. I read them out of interest at first and then started trying to understand the learnings from the mistakes or near misses by other pilots.

As I progressed and learnt more about flying, I started reaching out to other sources - YouTube, discussions with other pilots, overseas publications including the Flight Safety Magazine published by Australia's CASA.

Given New Zealand's close ties with the United Kingdom, I assumed their Civil Aviation Authority would be similar to New Zealand's, which is how I found CHIRP.

After talking with a good friend, and pilot, Ben Marcus from the United States, I asked him which reports he read and he suggested that I look at the FAA and their NASA CALLBACK news.

As I read more, I built up a mental picture - an understanding of how each country was unique and had diverse learnings. Some reports were very different but every story had a great takeaway I could learn from.

The reports in CALLBACK were very Air Transport focused, which is not covered in the reports published in New Zealand and only rarely mentioned in Australia. CHIRP split their reporting into General Aviation and Air Transport. The General Aviation stories had a large number of ATC and infringement stories, which again was lacking in New Zealand and Australia. I considered that maybe New Zealand and Australia have less controlled areas, but then again I have had a few close infringements myself but have never reported them.

My wife is an avid reader of books and an author, and with this influence I have been reading more. Kirsten has successfully published four books with another two currently underway. She suggested that I should look at publishing my own stories. Which expanded into thinking I could ask a few friends to share their stories. Then I decided to bring in the stories which helped me learn and improve.

CASA, NASA and CHIRP were all happy for their stories to be republished. Sadly that was not the case with New Zealand's CAA.

As I embarked on this project, I asked a number of experienced pilots what they wanted to read. Those conversations made it clear that the data needed to be split into two books - one covering General Aviation (this book), and one specifically for Air Transport - *101 Lessons From The Sky*, which will be published in late 2018.

In *81 Lessons from the Sky*, you'll read the stories and learn the lessons learnt by pilots from around the globe. Here's to safer flying.

Thank you

Fletcher McKenzie

HOW TO USE THIS BOOK

Each lesson has been replicated in the pilot's or crew member's words, without any editing other than minor grammatical corrections. You may notice some errors. We have purposely not amended the original reports.

A glossary of terms is included at the end of this book for your reference. Please note that this book may contain a mixture of both American English and British English, depending on who is telling the story.

If you find a term or an acronym in this book which isn't in the glossary, please email Fletcher:

fletch@avgasgroup.com

Each lesson has space for you to make your own notes if you want to. I recommend doing this to cement the learning.

Writing a short review of this book on your favourite digital platform, or on your personal blog or Facebook page, will help spread the word about aviation safety. Saving lives is the primary goal of this book.

AUSTRALIA - AUS - CASA

Flight Safety Australia:
Civil Aviation Safety Authority

CASA's flagship aviation safety magazine. Topical, technical, but reader-friendly, articles cover all the key aviation safety issues – safety management systems, maintenance, runway safety, human factors, airspace, training, aviation medicine – and more.

Flight Safety Australia, and its predecessor the Aviation Safety Digest, have provided the Australian aviation community with credible and comprehensive aviation safety information since the early 1950s.

From its beginnings as a printed monochrome booklet published only a few times a year, Flight Safety Australia has evolved into an interactive and content-rich publication available across multiple digital platforms.

The website and app keeps readers updated daily. Readers can also experience a stunning interactive digital magazine version for Android and iOS tablets, available by downloading the Flight Safety

Australia app from the relevant app stores. The magazine app is published bi-monthly.

Flight Safety Australia is produced by a small, dynamic team of writers, designers and contributors based out of the Safety Promotion branch of Australia's Civil Aviation Safety Authority. You can access previous issues of Flight Safety Australia online. For editions from 1996 through to April 2014.

Close Calls. The aviation community who have had a close call write to Close Calls about an aviation incident or accident that they have been involved in (as long as it's not the subject of a current official investigation). Written by CASA staff writers unless noted.

With permission, we selected a number of stories for this book.

www.flightsafetyaustralia.com

UNITED KINGDOM - UK - CHIRP

Confidential Human Factors Incident
Report Programme for Aviation

Known by the acronym CHIRP, its aim is to contribute to the enhancement of flight safety in the UK commercial and general aviation industries, by providing a totally independent confidential reporting system for all individuals employed in or associated with the industries.

The Programme is available to engineers and technical staff involved with the design and manufacturing processes, flight crew members, cabin crew members, air traffic controllers, licensed engineers and maintenance/engineering personnel and individual aircraft owners/operators.

CHIRP complements the UK's CAA Mandatory Occurrence Reporting system and other formal reporting systems operated by many UK organisations, by providing a means by which individuals are able to raise safety-related issues of concern without being identified to their peer group, management, or the Regulatory Authority.

CHIRP is a totally independent programme for the collection of confidential safety data, and when appropriate, acting or advising on information gained through confidential reports. Independent advice is provided on aeromedical and Human Factors aspects of reports, involving such topics as errors, fatigue, poor ergonomics, management pressures, deficiencies in communication or team performance. The sensitivity of these topics requires that the anonymity of the reporter must be, and always has been, fully protected.

The CHIRP organisation is comprised of a small team of specialists with professional and technical expertise in commercial aviation and Human Factors. The Programmes are also able to draw on the assistance of a wide range of individual experts and specialist bodies across the spectrum of aviation and maritime sciences in order to promote the resolution of issues raised.

CHIRP® reports are published as a contribution to safety in the aviation industry. FEEDBACK is published quarterly and is circulated in several GA publications throughout the UK.

With permission, we selected a number of stories for this book.

www.chirp.co.uk

UNITED STATES OF AMERICA - USA - ASRS

Aviation Safety Reporting System

ASRS collects voluntarily submitted aviation safety incident/situation reports from pilots, controllers, and others. It then analyses, and responds to the voluntarily submitted aviation safety incident reports in order to lessen the likelihood of aviation accidents.

ASRS acts on the information these reports contain. It identifies system deficiencies, and issues alerting messages to persons in a position to correct them. It educates through its newsletter CALLBACK, its journal ASRS Directline and through its research studies. Its database is a public repository which serves the FAA and NASA's needs and those of other organisations world-wide which are engaged in research and the promotion of safe flight.

ASRS data are used to identify deficiencies and discrepancies in the National Aviation System (NAS) so that these can be remedied by appropriate authorities. Support policy formulation and planning for, and improvements to, the NAS. Strengthen the foundation of aviation human factors safety research. This is particularly important since it is generally conceded that over two-thirds of all aviation accidents and incidents have their roots in human performance errors.

ASRS's award winning publication CALLBACK is a monthly safety newsletter, which includes de-identified ASRS report excerpts with supporting commentary in a popular "lessons learned" format. In addition, CALLBACK may contain features on ASRS research studies and related aviation safety information. Editorial use and reproduction of CALLBACK articles is encouraged. ASRS appreciates any appropriate attribution of this information. ASRS thanks the aviation community for its interest in and support of CALLBACK.

With permission, we selected a number of stories for this book.

www.asrs.arc.nasa.gov

CHAPTER 1

AIRWORTHINESS & MAINTENANCE

"Accuracy means something to me. It's vital to my sense of values. I've learned not to trust people who are inaccurate. Every aviator knows that if mechanics are inaccurate, aircraft crash. If pilots are inaccurate, they get lost — sometimes killed. In my profession life itself depends on accuracy."

Charles A. Lindbergh

DRINKING DISTRACTION
CASA

Name withheld by request, Sep 6, 2017

It was my rostered day as tow pilot at the gliding club. I got there early so I could pre-flight the Pawnee and prepare everything in good time before the briefing. The weather was looking great. One of those beautiful winter days with clear blue skies and great visibility.

I checked the aircraft over thoroughly in the hangar and everything seemed fine. Fuelled and oiled I strolled over to the clubroom for the daily briefing. It looked like an ideal day for a tow pilot—nice weather, not too busy and not too hot (unlike summer!).

After the daily briefing I strolled back to my car next to the hangar and collected my headset, kneeboard and my camelbak hydration pack to put them into the aircraft. The camelback went in its usual place on the parcel shelf behind my head. I left the headset on the seat ready. I pulled the Pawnee out of the hangar, hooked up the rope and waited till the first glider looked ready to launch, then I started the engine.

As it was the first flight of the day I did a full magneto and power check before take-off and all appeared normal. I taxied into position in front of the glider, did my pre-take-off checks, moved the stick around the four corners to check 'controls full and free', took up the slack in the rope and then we were off. Full power, keeping straight with rudder, let the tail lift, and then airborne. A few gentle turns and at 3000 ft the glider released.

Good lookout, power reduced, left turn to give separation from the glider and then back to the airfield for the next tow. As I turned onto finals the picture ahead looked good for the approach.

I reached down with my hand for the flap lever which is a handbrake-style lever on the left cockpit floor. Depressing the button I pulled the lever up to select the first stage. Part way up I felt a solid restriction and the lever wouldn't go any further. I could feel it wasn't locked correctly in position so I pulled it a bit harder to try and get it to lock. The restriction felt even greater the more I pulled. After several more attempts it still wasn't moving.

The picture out of the front windscreen started to look like I was getting too high, but with one hand still on the flap lever and one on the stick I didn't have a spare to reduce the throttle. The aircraft continued along finals.

What to do now? I slowly released the flap lever back to the floor. The lever moved down all the way as it should and the flaps stayed locked up. Now I had a spare hand for the throttle.

At this stage what I should have done is performed a go-around and done a simple flap-less landing. What I actually did was reduce the throttle to idle in order to correct the rapidly developing overshoot, point the nose down and tried the flaps again. Same problem. Jammed whenever I got the lever part-way up. I tried again with more force but still it did not work.

I glanced down just to make sure I had the correct lever (this particular Pawnee also had a similar positioned lever for spraying) and yes, I had the correct lever but what I noticed was the blue pipe of my camelback leading down to the flap lever.

I immediately knew what had happened.

I always carried a Camelbak™ in the cockpit while towing to stay hydrated as often there was little time for a drink stop on a busy day. I usually left the pipe dangling down from the rear parcel shelf on the left side close to my elbow so I could grab it during a turnaround and have a quick drink. The long pipe must have dropped completely down and got caught in the flap lever.

With no flaps an overshoot was now looking likely but I still persisted with trying to get the flaps down. I ran my hand down the Camelbak™ pipe and pulled it as hard as I could. Finally it came free. I then grabbed the flap lever from the floor and pulled it up. It worked perfectly and I took both stages of flap at once.

My attention returned to the front of the aircraft and I realised that I wasn't going to make the runway as I was much too high. I applied full power and went around. But in my rush I left the flaps down. In this case it didn't really matter as the Pawnee had masses of extra power. I realised when turning crosswind the flaps were still down and rapidly raised them.

The following circuit and landing were uneventful but I was glad to get back on the ground. As I taxied back the next glider was ready. I taxied briefly off the runway to check the flap lever and as I looked down I noticed the cockpit floor was wet. I pulled on the drinking tube again and realised the bite valve on the end was missing. It must have been that which jammed in the flap lever and when I pulled it came off. I quickly located it on the cockpit floor, reinserted it into the tube and stowed it all on the parcel shelf this time well out of the way of the flap lever. The rest of the days towing was uneventful.

So what did I learn in those seconds which seemed like a lifetime?

Check controls full and free means all flight controls, including flaps. Do it before every flight because you never know what might be in the way.

I had checked the flap operation fully during the daily inspection but at that point my camelback was still in the car so they moved freely. If I had done it prior to take-off I would have had the problem on the ground.

Always fly the aeroplane. Don't get distracted and especially not on approach or when low. If in doubt go around, climb higher and troubleshoot the problem at altitude.

Practice your flapless landings. One day you might need to do one for real.

And don't forget to stay hydrated!

NOTES:

SEAT FAILURE ON TAKE-OFF

CHIRP

May 2017, Issue 72

On Sunday 16 October 2016 a Cessna 150 crashed at Bourn airfield on take-off and I sent a text to my flying partner saying that I thought it could be the classic case of seat lock failure. This is where the seat lock is not fully engaged and as the pilot rotates it can rush back. The pilot hangs onto the yoke and the aircraft pitches up, stalls and spins in.

The following weekend we both arrived at the airfield and again discussed the possible reason for the crash. We checked out my Cessna [ ] and prepared for start-up. As I am aware of the seat failure situation, I always lock the pin in place and then "rattle" the seat back and forth to check that it is locked.

We taxied out to the warm up area and I carried out my pre-flight checks. Again as part of my checks I "rattled" the seat. I then lined up on the runway, did a few more checks and opened the throttle. As I approached takeoff speed I rotated the aircraft and when we were about 10 feet off the ground, my seat suddenly shot backwards. My arms were at full stretch and I could not reach the rudder pedals or the throttle (I am short).

My co-pilot shouted at me "Nose Down!" and I shouted back "Take Control! He pushed the yoke forward and the aircraft wallowed then went downwards picking up speed. We cleared the runway and climbed out and he asked what had happened.

We did a circuit and I asked him if he was OK landing from the right seat and he said "Possibly!" Not a good answer, so I pulled my seat forward and locked the pin again. I noticed that it did not have any tension from the spring that pulls it downwards and keeps it in place. We decided that I would land the aircraft but he would follow me through and take control for a go around if necessary. I landed OK and taxied back to the ramp.

Upon examination, we found that the spring had broken and was hanging on one point. I took out the spring and thought I would check how bad the spring was. I got a pair of pliers to bend the top of the spring which snapped off. I bent another bit and that snapped off. The spring which I assume was the same age as the aircraft as it was painted the same colour as the seat (51 years), was completely metal fatigued.

Lessons Learned:

I have now changed both front seat springs but it has occurred to me that the springs have a limited life and they should perhaps be replaced over a certain period, say 10 years. Unfortunately, Cessna charge £25 for each spring which may discourage owners to replace them at regular intervals.

A further point is that we as pilots who often fly as P2 should practise flying from the right seat in case of emergency, especially landing and in a crosswind. The situation is so different from what one is used to.

Even though the accident the week previously was fresh in my mind, my seat rushing back still came as a shock and if my co-pilot had not taken control immediately, the situation could have been very much worse.

CHIRP Comment: Loss of control incidents are reportable as Mandatory Occurrence Reports (MORs) and this reporter had complied with the requirement. Since seat slippage can occur on any aircraft with a moveable seat, it is vital to check the security of the seat, as this pilot did, whether or not the seat has recently been moved. Although the incident was caused by a failure of the lock pin spring, there is a history of problems with other aspects of the seat and a relevant and extant FAA Airworthiness Directive FAA AD 2011-10-09 that applies to many models of Cessna aircraft. The summary extract says:

> "SUMMARY: We are superseding an existing airworthiness directive (AD) for Cessna Aircraft Company (Cessna) 150, 152, 170, 172, 175, 177, 180, 182, 185, 188, 190, 195, 206, 207, 210, T303, 336, and 337 series airplanes. That AD currently requires repetitive inspections and replacement of parts, if necessary, of the seat rail and seat rail holes; seat pin engagement; seat rollers, washers, and axle bolts or bushings; wall thickness of roller housing and the tang; and lock pin springs. This new AD requires retaining all of the actions from the previous AD and adding steps to the inspection procedures in the previous AD. This AD was prompted by added steps to the inspection procedures, added revised figures, and clarification of some of the existing steps. We are issuing this AD to prevent seat slippage or the seat roller housing from departing the seat rail, which may consequently cause the pilot/co-pilot to be unable to reach all the controls. This failure could lead to the pilot/co-pilot losing control of the airplane."

It should be noted that the FAA AD 2011-10-09 inspections and any actions arising (cleaning, replacement due to wear, cracking etc.) should continue to be performed every 12 months or every 100 HR TIS, whichever comes sooner, and the work should be carried out by a qualified aircraft engineer.

AUTHOR UPDATE: 9 JULY 2018

Thanks to two pilots (Rob and Simon) I found the following update from Cessna:

Service Bulletin SEB07-5 Revision 6, Pilot and Copilot Secondary Seat Stop Installation is extended to December 31, 2018.
www.support.cessna.com

I still have my SAF-T-STOP and carry it with me, as I jump into various Cessna aircraft.

NOTES:

PRE-FLIGHT CHECK FAILURE

CHIRP

Nov 2016, Issue 70

I arrived at the airfield at midday to clean my flexwing microlight and do some local flying. My co-owner was already there having flown in the morning. To clean the wing we decided to "hobble" the aircraft. This involved removing the front strut from the trike (held in place by clevis pins and safety rings) and lowering the wing. We then cleaned the wing and applied sun protection spray. This done, we raised the wing with some little difficulty and I replaced the front strut. My co-owner then departed.

Another flying buddy had arrived and we decided to fly together to a local strip. I quickly pre-flighted the aircraft, started up and performed my pre-take off checks at the hold point. My buddy had already taken off but landed just as I was completing my checks to tell me that our planned route was looking murky, and suggested an alternative. He then took off and I followed shortly afterwards.

As the aircraft took off, I felt the control bar movement was unusual, glanced up and saw that I hadn't replaced the top clevis pin and the strut had now detached from the pylon. I performed an immediate emergency landing, made a lot simpler by having a long WWII concrete runway available straight ahead.

Lessons Learned:

There are a number of lessons I've learned from this rather humbling experience, where there were three opportunities to spot the error before flight.

1 Given that there were two of us cleaning the wing, we should have taken the opportunity to have each other double-check our work to spot errors when we raised the wing.

2 As my co-owner had already performed the daily inspection of the aircraft, I performed a much shorter check in my pre-flight. Subconsciously I was rushing - I specifically remember telling myself to slow down. I should have considered that "hobbling" the aircraft meant the aircraft had been re-rigged and a full daily inspection was needed before flight.

3 I was distracted by my buddy landing as I was completing my pre take-off checks.

4 The pre-take off check mnemonic I use (and I understand is still taught in the NPPL (M) flexwing syllabus) is CHIEF TAP [C=Controls, H=Harness, I=Instruments, E= Engine, F=Fuel and T=Trims and Pins, A=All Clear, P=Power]. The problem is the "T" for "Trim and Pins". On my particular aircraft setting takeoff trim takes more than 10 seconds using an electric switch. The length of time and the positive action associated with "trim" made it easy to forget "and pins". In future I will separate the two items (CHIEF TPAP?), and I wonder if these checks could be separated more explicitly in the syllabus?

5 I had previously taken off with the trim not set properly, resulting in a particularly exciting take-off and so was particularly focussed on ensuring that trim was set. In future I should ensure that I don't focus on avoiding the last mistake I made.

CHIRP Comment: The front strut is a vital structural part of the airframe. There has been a fatality when a front strut connection failed and the aircraft broke up in straight and level flight. The reporter is congratulated for immediately landing straight ahead and so avoiding a serious accident.

The reporter has correctly identified the factors that contributed to this occurrence: lack of an independent check of the rigging, rushing and distraction. Flexwing microlight operators could perhaps learn from the gliding community where distraction during rigging is a recognised problem. To avoid interruptions during rigging, some gliding sites have adopted the wearing of a 'rigging hat' - a recognisable and conspicuous piece of headgear to warn anyone in the vicinity not to interrupt or otherwise distract the wearer because he/she is engaged in rigging an aircraft.

We should not rely on an aircraft remaining as it was during the daily inspection, especially if de-rigging is possible. The pre-flight checks should be constructed and carried out in such a way as to be able to identify any changes. Daily inspections and pre-flight checks should never be rushed; they should always be done thoroughly. The NPPL syllabus does not contain any suggested or required check sequences. The BMAA Instructor and Examiner Guide does suggest some check lists but it is up to each instructor to pass on checks that they feel are suitable for the aircraft type and circumstances.

NOTES:

SPEED TAPE FOR REPAIRS

CHIRP

May 2016, Issue 68

I was very surprised to see the photographs on the Internet of an engineer utilising speed tape around an engine nacelle to close a gap and therefore reduce vibration. I also see that it was being used on flap repairs. This tape made by 3M on their data sheet claims that the 425 and 426 variety can be used for aircraft repair. I have seen this tape in our consumable cupboard but have never seen it being used on airframes as a temporary repair as the tape does not have an approval or batch number on it. It has a FAR flammability rating but I was very intrigued when I saw the photos of it being used on an aircraft. Would love to know how you would certify this type of repair for flight as 3M as far as I can remember do not issue a batch or approval number for this product.

Look forward to your comments on this and only hope it is not an industry standard as I have never seen it mentioned in chapter 20.

CHIRP Comment: Metallised adhesive tape has been used to carry out temporary repairs on aircraft on nonstructural applications for many years. Typical applications are to cover up minor impact damage on tertiary (non load-bearing) panels until a permanent repair can be effected. It can be used in some instances on flying controls (e.g. flap trailing edges) where cracks in the composite structure have appeared and to prevent moisture ingress, freezing at altitude and further damage. It is not intended for long-term repair and damage should be properly assessed. Although regarded as a consumable, speed tape should still have a batch number to show its provenance.

NOTES:

STANDARD OF WORK
CHIRP

Nov 2015, Issue 66

I am writing on behalf of the engineering staff at [ ] and their concern about engineering standards. At present an annual check is being carried out by a licensed engineer on a [ ] in a private, non 145-approved hanger with no workshop manuals or up-to-date paperwork referencing any service bulletins ADs etc. The other worry is the standard of work is well below what is expected. The concerns of the staff are, if none of the engineering staff are involved in the maintenance or can even see the standard of work, who is to say an acceptable job is being undertaken knowing what poor standards are allowed in the maintenance hangar.

CHIRP Comment: An Aircraft Continuing Airworthiness Monitoring (ACAM) inspection determined that engineering standards at the reported facility were acceptable. The aircraft had since been moved to a different facility for Airworthiness Directive and final certification work. The assumption that because the work was not being conducted in a Part 145 hangar, the engineer did not have access to appropriate manuals proved to be incorrect. As it turned out, the aircraft concerned was an 'Annex II' type that did not fall under Part 145 regulations. All that said, the reporter was correct to raise his concerns. Although the inspection did not substantiate the reported shortcomings, the concerns were investigated; in other circumstances a similar report could highlight significant safety issues.

NOTES:

FRYING TONIGHT

CASA

by staff writers, Mar 28, 2014

There are some situations in flying that really energise your thinking. Think of engine failure. Think of weather conditions deteriorating below minimums. And, as I recently discovered, the smell of something burning just moments after take-off.

The morning's solo flight from Griffith to my home base in Canberra promised to be routine. The met briefing was for a light westerly tailwind and a mid-level cloud base well above the LSALT. No worries there.

There was a local NOTAM 'Bird hazard exists due to locust plague'. 'OK', I thought, 'I need to look out for the birds'.

As I walked out to the Arrow, a local ag pilot drove up. He was getting ready for a day of spraying as the farmers had been taking a hammering from the swarming insects.

'What's it like flying around the locusts?' I asked.

'Need to stay above the big swarms,' he advised, 'but keep an eye on the oil temp, as the little buggers can plug up your oil cooler.' Good bit of local knowledge, I thought.

With the flight plan in the system and pre-flight completed, it was time to fly. At the holding point, I went through my checklist. An instructor once told me that a checklist is always a work in progress. Mine has grown from the original (BUMFISH) to a current two-page incarnation that would make a NASA mission controller proud.

The section on engine failure on take-off I usually recite out loud:

Fly the plane (maintain 90kt)

Find the field (options restricted to 30 degrees left or right)

Figure out the approach (straight ahead)

Fix or isolate the problem (time permitting)

Phone a friend (call ATC)

Fuel and electrics shutdown

Flee the aircraft (take the EPIRB and grab bag, two door latches to open, exit, and move upwind)

So far, no passengers have asked to deplane after my monologue, but it has raised a few eyebrows.

With the checklist complete, it was time to taxi out. There was the occasional locust on the runway, but what could the odd insect do to an aircraft, I asked myself.

A lot, as I was about to find out.

The ground roll was routine. A quick instrument check as the plane accelerated showed all was normal. Rotate at 60 kt, gear up and trim for 90 kt – so far so good. Passing through 300 ft AGL, I noticed a burning smell. Slight at first, but rapidly becoming more intense.

My first reaction was disbelief. (Others would later call this my moment of denial.) Then the adrenalin kicked in. The plane was flying OK, but obviously I had a problem. Most likely a fire, but where?

Should I do an immediate landing straight ahead (as per my engine failure rehearsal)? It has been drilled into all of us never to turn back if there is an engine failure. But the instrument readings were all normal. The engine sounded okay and felt strong.

Would a better option be an immediate turn back to the aerodrome and a precautionary landing? A precautionary landing that would require an unrehearsed low-level circuit at an unfamiliar aerodrome. What if the engine stopped on the way back? Would the extra minute or two in the air create a truly flaming Arrow? Obstacles? Traffic? My focus was starting to narrow...

It was time to stop dithering and start doing.

A rapid return to the aerodrome and a precautionary landing seemed the best option.

During my last flight review, Ben, my examiner, had gone through a new CASA learning module that reviewed the effect of distractions on aviation safety. Plenty to distract me here, I thought.

'Just fly the plane.' my inner voices kept reminding me. 'And remember to get the gear down.'

Well, that was your culprit.

A locust. They don't smell real flash when they are cooking.'

Time to phone a friend. A quick call to Melbourne Centre to advise them of the change of plan. The controller's response was brief.

'What's the nature of your problem?'

'Something's burning.'

'Copy,' he replied, 'Report operations normal in five minutes. Out.'

What followed was a very tight circuit, a normal (wheels down) landing, an Ops Normal call to Centre ... and then a few extremely deep breaths.

Going over the aircraft revealed nothing out of the ordinary – no oil or fuel leaks, no visible smoke or scorch marks around the engine. It was time to call Rob, my LAME.

He directed me to the cabin air intake on the engine cowling, where ram air is directed over the exhaust system.

'Can you see a bit of soot on the exhaust manifold? About 2cm long?' he asked.

'Yes'

'Well, that was your culprit. A locust. They don't smell real flash when they are cooking.' (Rob's a country boy.)

The flight back to Canberra was far less eventful.

Thinking back, I realised that while I had rehearsed for a complete engine failure after take-off, I had no mental script for the possibility of a return and precautionary landing. The issues of circuit direction, local obstacles, built-up areas, conflicting traffic and a compressed time for landing checks could all have been reviewed on the ground beforehand.

A new section on precautionary landings now graces my (ever-expanding) pre take-off checklist.

I also understood the hidden benefit of notifying Centre when things are not going well. Obviously there was little that the controller could do for me in the cockpit. But a few calm words and knowing that 'The System' was swinging into action was hugely reassuring. Sometimes that is all that is needed to prevent a difficult situation becoming something worse.

I now know that a 30gm insect can compromise the safety of a 1200kg aircraft, and I am also pretty certain that locusts will not be featuring on a Master Chef menu any time soon.

NOTES:

PROPERLY CLEAR OF THE PROP?
CASA

by Phillip Zamagias, Mar 28, 2014

How many times have we been told 'treat every propeller as if it is live'?

Like many things in aviation, years of doing repetitive tasks with no apparent danger can breed a familiarity that must never be allowed to overshadow good training.

Learning how to be a bush pilot in the Northern Territory, I was shown how to handle a propeller with due care. I was also shown how to 'hand start' an engine should the need ever arise. Good stuff!

Many years later, having never hand swung a prop to start an engine, or had an engine fire up unexpectedly, I came within a whisker of being 'sliced and diced'.

While getting ready for an early departure from a remote bush airstrip, I began the very familiar routine of a daily inspection on my recently acquired plane. It was a near-new Piper 6XT with glass cockpit.

I had less than 100 hours on type, but more than 3500hrs on Cessna-206s, which had formed the mainstay of my bush flying career. The Piper brought with it a significant change in ergonomics that almost cost me dearly.

Not only were the cockpit instruments a radical departure from the F and G-model Cessna 206s I had traversed the country in, but the ignition switches were very different.

In single-engine Cessna's the ignition is operated by a key. On shutdown a pilot typically performs a magneto check before reducing the mixture control to idle cut-off. Once the engine has stopped, the key is rotated to the 'ignition off' position and the key is removed. Simple.

Having the keys in your pocket, especially when you are the sole pilot and away from home base, gives you a feeling of security. Of course, there is always the chance of a magneto going open-circuit and therefore being live. That's why we are told to treat every propeller as live.

In the Piper, the ignition switches are conveniently located on the eyebrow panel above the pilot's head. A proper shutdown check would ensure that the switches are in the 'Off' position after the engine is shut down.

I clearly missed that part of the checklist on shutdown and before starting the pre-flight for the next day's trip. The friend I had been visiting came out to the airstrip and was filming my pre-flight in preparation for a close-up shot of takeoff.

What Richard saw shocked him almost as much as it did me.

As I checked the propeller's leading edges for stone damage and pulled one blade through compression, the engine fired!

I felt the blade just graze my forearm and narrowly miss my head. Not enough to break any skin or leave a mark, but enough for me to feel the proximity of the blade.

My reaction is obvious from the video clip. I ran!

As this close call shows, every propeller can potentially bite. Treat every prop as if it's live and stay well away whenever possible.

I was surprisingly calm in the presence of my friend and the passenger who was coming with me on the next flight. I dismissed it with the calm detachment of a professional pilot and soldiered on.

Six years later I have given up flying and have been reflecting on that incident. I am submitting this article as a means of sharing what I learned that day.

Firstly, it can happen to you. Always maintain an attitude of vigilance and safety so that if (and when) something goes wrong, it doesn't have to spell disaster.

Secondly, be extra careful when changing aircraft type, especially when changing manufacturers. Some basics carry over from model to model, but there are often significant differences in standard operating procedures across different brands of aircraft or engines. Take, for example, the use of fuel pumps in high-wing and low-wing aircraft.

Thirdly, no matter how comfortable you feel about your aeroplane, use checklists for shutdown and do a safety check before starting a pre-flight on an aeroplane. You might have missed something or, if it is a line aircraft, someone else might have left the switches in an unsafe position.

Finally, every propeller can potentially bite. Make sure you never have any body parts (or anyone else's) in the arc of a propeller. Stand clear and be ready to jump away should the engine fire up.

I attribute my miraculous escape to the subliminal residue of the training I had received many years ago that just made me wary of any propeller.

However it was also something of a miracle that day.

Maybe God isn't finished with me yet?

NOTES:

BIRD DOG DISTRACTION

CASA

by staff writers, Mar 25, 2014

Distraction by a fellow pilot's skills caused this embarrassed aviator to review his limitations.

The Cessna 305, or Bird Dog, made its debut overhead the jungles during the Vietnam War. I was excited to be flying this aircraft for my first paid flying job. Boy was I rapt!

Inspections of power lines and the vegetation surrounding them were made from a few hundred feet above ground level. Early morning flying was magnificent, with slivers of orange sunlight peeping over the horizon and the pristine crisp autumn air of outback NSW. Inspecting powerlines has to be one of the most challenging, demanding and exciting jobs around.

Tailwheel Cessna's that have not been ground looped are rare in Australia, so my chief pilot made sure I had a thorough checkout in the machine so as not to add to the statistics.

The start of my first day went well. With the first two sorties going to plan, and after four hours of flying, I was feeling a little less tense. After a bite to eat, it was time to head back to base. I went to top up the oil as the old Continental engine was a little thirsty. Opening the cowls, I removed the locking pin on the oil filler cap and started to pour in a litre of oil. Just at that moment a glider commenced a winch launch close by, and climbed out in front of me at an impressive angle. 'Wow, that looks cool', I thought as I finished topping up the oil and then closed and fastened the cowls, with their locking pins facing rearwards.

Start up; the usual company pre-take-off checks were completed without any abnormal readings, a thumbs up from my observer in the back and smoothly and gently, I applied full power, my feet finely see-sawing the rudder pedals to make a good quality take-off for a budding amateur. Departure track was 175 degrees and cruising altitude was 1500 feet. I smoothly rolled left onto departure heading while passing over the rural township.

Unknown to me were the droplets of black oil tracing my departure from the parking bay. After ten more minutes of spraying oil droplets across the countryside, my oil pressure gauge thought it was time to let me know what was happening by dropping into the red. I quickly glanced to the side of it, but the oil temperature was only slightly higher than normal.

Then I craned my head against the Perspex window, and my heart sank.

Slick glistening black oil covered the left wheel and strut. (During my initial checkout I had been told that in the unlikely event of the oil filler cap being left off, the C305 would not siphon the oil onto the windscreen like most Cessna's, but would deposit it outside the cowls onto the fuselage and left gear leg.)

What an idiot! I had left the oil cap off the engine after topping up. My immediate thoughts were: Where shall I land? How long have I been flying? How long do I have before my engine stops? I will lose my job! What is my rear observer going to think?

Automatically, I reduced power to not much more than idle, and chose a slightly upward sloping sheep paddock among the gentle rolling hills to put the Bird Dog down. After landing, the sheep quickly gathered at an inquisitive distance to see this red and white oily-looking machine, with a very red-faced pilot to match. I quickly topped up the oil with the four-litre bottle in the rear of the aircraft kept (obviously) for the occasion. After checking that everything was back in place and oil cap on, I took off and flew back to base. The remainder of the trip was flown in silence. The boss was definitely not impressed, but thankfully did not fire me.

Some reflections on my flying that day:

When I was filling up the oil, I was distracted by the glider launching. I shut the cowls up and put their pins back in place, but didn't check the oil filler cap.

After I jumped back in to take off from the paddock, I noticed I had left in such a flap that I had left the master and the mags on.

Fatigue. It had been a very early start and now was well past lunch. I make more mistakes when I am tired, and therefore need to be extra vigilant, or just not fly.

After landing in the paddock I should have talked to the chief pilot before flying again.

What would the outcome have been if I had been flying over ocean, forest or mountains?

This incident was one of the best things to happen to me in aviation. It highlighted several things, as well as lowering my pride a notch or two. Since that day I have made a habit of doing a thorough inspection of my aircraft before I take to the air. Twelve years later, after flying over foreign countries, inhospitable deserts, oceans and dense jungles, I am thankful for the lessons learnt over the sheep paddock that day.

NOTES:

CHAPTER 2
COMPLACENCY & FATIGUE

"In flying I have learned that carelessness and overconfidence are usually far more dangerous than deliberately accepted risks."
Wilbur Wright
(in a letter to his father, September 1900)

PUSH THE 'RIGHT' PEDAL

CALLBACK

Jan 2016, Issue 432

I was flying ... at 11,000 feet on an IFR flight plan. My autopilot disconnected and revealed an out-of-trim condition which caused the aircraft to yaw to the left. I had stretched my right leg to the right of the cockpit for comfort. When the aircraft yawed, I instinctively pressed my right foot on the rudder pedal. This caused the aircraft to yaw even more to the left, requiring full right aileron to keep from rolling inverted. I turned the autopilot off and released the rudder trim with no effect. I also reduced power and lowered the nose to get better control, advising ATC that I was turning and descending with a flight control problem. ATC advised me that [an airport] was ahead about ten miles.... As I continued to troubleshoot, I noticed that my right foot was pressing on the copilot left rudder pedal instead of the pilot right rudder pedal. As soon as I got my foot on the correct rudder pedal, I was able to control the aircraft and advised ATC. I continued the flight.

NOTES:

EVENT AT A BUSY FLY-IN

CHIRP

May 2015, Issue 64

The event took place during a busy "Fly-in" event at a UK GA aerodrome that provides an aerodrome flight information service. The weather was good VMC and there was a brisk breeze which, as well as giving a good head-wind component for approach, also gave a noticeable crosswind from the right and associated turbulence. A right hand circuit was in use and it was busy. I flew a completely standard overhead join and when on the downwind leg I saw two aircraft ahead, one on short finals and the second just beginning its final approach. The spacing looked just right for me. Following my "downwind to land" R/T call I was told to "report finals" which I subsequently did and then, once the aircraft ahead had vacated the runway, was invited to "land at my discretion". I flew a continuous descending final turn and my approach and landing was completely normal; I was able to vacate the runway in sufficient time for the following aircraft to be able to land. All seemed to be working well, but when established on my final approach I did hear one aircraft behind me calling that he was "going around." It was not until more than an hour after my landing that I was approached by another pilot and it transpired that he was the one that I had heard call "going around." The reason for this was that, having extended his downwind leg to increase spacing from the aircraft ahead, he was flying a longish flat approach to the runway when my aircraft appeared just in front and above him whereupon he, in order to avoid collision, manoeuvred to the dead side and went around. I never saw his aircraft! Suffice to say I was mortified, embarrassed and very sorry for not seeing the other aircraft -and I still am.

Lessons Learned:

Much has been written and taught over the years about the importance of listening-out and looking-out, all of it correct, but in a very busy non-controlled aerodrome environment to keep track of all the aircraft is very difficult and we all realise the limitations of lookout. However, having said that, I have thought long and hard about any lessons that I and others could glean from this incident and I have identified two main points that could be of use in reducing the chances of this type of Airprox (air proximity) from reoccurring.

I flew a continuous turn onto final approach since it was more convenient to do given the tightening crosswind, it would help the pilots following me achieve spacing and it is as I was taught to do in the RAF. However, RAF circuits are never as busy as the one at the fly-in when my Airprox occurred and they are always controlled by an ATC tower controller. Whilst in the continuous final turn an aircraft is belly-up and therefore its pilot blind to any traffic on a longer straight-in approach, something that would be announced were full ATC in attendance. Therefore, a conventional "square" circuit that features a straight descending base leg gives the pilot the opportunity to perform a further visual check that the straight-in approach is clear of traffic before turning onto final approach and it is certainly something that I will always do in future when operating in a busy visual circuit.

The practice of extending the downwind leg to achieve spacing from traffic ahead does cause problems. The first is that an aircraft performing such an extension places itself in a position in which it is not expected to be in by other pilots and, as happened in the subject incident, the chances of it being visually acquired by them are reduced. The second is that following aircraft have their circuit geometry compromised by the extending aircraft and they are either obliged to follow the extending aircraft (providing they can see it) or to go around. An RAF rule that I was taught was that, unless advised by ATC, the downwind leg should never be extended and that a go-around be flown if spacing from traffic ahead is insufficient, spacing properly being achieved at the upwind part of the circuit by adjusting the position at which the crosswind turn is made. The cause of this Airprox was my failure to see and avoid the other aircraft, but the consideration at A and B above may reduce the chances of the happening again.

CHIRP Comment: We are grateful to the reporter for his open report and thorough analysis of this occurrence. It is important to fly in accordance with the established circuit pattern and the operation being conducted. Military circuits with a continuous turn from the end of downwind on to final are not compatible with civilian circuits; as the reporter notes, the continuous turn makes it difficult to look for aircraft on an extended final and the timing of the "final" call on the RT, made as the aircraft 'tips in' from downwind, will cause confusion. Therefore it was essential to fly civilian 'square' circuits at this event. The reporter is also correct to note that extending downwind can cause problems in the visual circuit, particularly where the circuits extend beyond the boundaries of the ATZ! If a circuit is becoming over extended, the option of going around from the end of downwind allows it to be tightened up again.

NOTES:

MEA CULPA

CHIRP

May 2015, Issue 64

I am an experienced glider pilot and consider myself to be pretty 'switched on' in just about every situation. The reason I begin with this statement is that it may be contributory to the incident that I just got away with - by the skin of my teeth! I have been a "hobby pilot" and have around 4000 hours as pilot in command. I fly gliders mostly but also have a share in a touring motor glider (TMG). I also have a PPL. The [ ] is a tail wheel aircraft but the main wheels are retractable. Previously I had a share in another TMG that has a fixed undercarriage but in many other ways is quite similar. I have used the experience gained to good effect in the [current aircraft] and this may also be relevant to this incident. On the day in question, the wind was ten knots from around 30 degrees across the runway with gusts to fifteen knots that made the x-wind component even worse. It was also just beginning to become thermic.

The airfield is on the top of a ridge with down slopes either side of the airfield. The grass runway itself is not flat but slopes up at either end. As a glider pilot, I am aware of the risk of turbulence, curl over and excessive sink when flying behind the top of a ridge and this concern was a major part of my workload as I flew the approach. I had flown into [ ] on several previous occasions but not for some years. On every previous occasion, I have landed on the reciprocal runway. Another contributory factor was that from my perspective, the runway in use appeared to slope upwards. I was concerned that my aircraft would not have sufficient take-off performance to take-off in a strong x-wind on an uphill runway. I actually queried with [ ] Radio if there was a significant slope in the runway. The third factor in this incident is that the circuit was busy. I prefer to fly glider style circuits with a steep 'half airbrake' approach. I had to conform to the GA circuit traffic and fly a long flat approach. I have never quite understood why the GA community adopts this procedure since if the engine were to stop whilst on approach, there would be little chance of actually gliding a light aircraft to the runway threshold. I did my downwind checks as usual and configured the engine for a possible go-around. To do this, I opened the cowl flap, selected the propeller pitch to fine and switched on the fuel booster pump. For the life of me, I cannot think why I neglected to lower the wheels at this stage. This is where my own 'conceit' must have had a hand. I skimped on the checks! I was also flying it like [my previous TMG] - big mistake! Having turned base and then set up for a long, low final approach, I didn't use the airbrakes. The aircraft has a warning buzzer in the cockpit that sounds if the airbrakes are extended and the main wheels are not lowered. It also sounds when the gear is in transit and unlocked. In all other cases, I would use around half airbrake on approach but this approach was so flat, I didn't need to use any airbrake. At the final part of the approach, I was so focussed on staying on the centre line that I completely filtered out the warning buzzer when I finally opened the airbrakes. I rounded out and was expecting the wheels to touch. It was not until I was actually lower to the ground than is normal with the gear down that I realised that I had neglected to lower the gear. I applied full throttle and closed the brakes. I must have been literally one second away from striking the prop on the ground. I shakily called that I was going round and the second attempt to land was all normal. Unfortunately for me, [ ] was busy that day and I seemed to have a large audience watching me. I am still very sheepish about this. On numerous occasions I have read of gliding incidents where pilots land with the main wheel still retracted and thought that I am far too switched on to do something daft like that.

Well, I nearly did it myself and now see that factors were:

1. Flying an aircraft that is very similar to one previously owned. Operating procedures do not translate exactly.
2. A very high workload due to difficult cross wind and risk of curl over.
3. An unfamiliar circuit and worries about runway slope for later departure.
4. Flying a type of circuit that I do not like to fly.
5. Overconfidence in my own competence and experience. I was complacent about flying the [ ] and clearly did not do the checks well enough. In actual fact the later departure from [ ] was absolutely fine, despite my earlier concerns about the slope in the runway.

Lessons Learned:

When flying different, but otherwise similar aircraft, focus more on differences training. Normally, an experienced [ ] pilot could get into a [ ] and fly it without any major problem. Do not "skimp" checks. Don't become complacent through over confidence. Aeroplanes bite fools and I was extremely lucky to have got away with it!

CHIRP Comment: Another very honest report that brings out several Human Factors issues. The reporter mentions overconfidence but the issue could be under-arousal. There are 3 stages of pilot experience that all have their own hazards; the first stage is that the workload is too high for the pilot's experience, followed by the experimental stage and finally the stage where the workload does not provide sufficient arousal for the immediate task in hand. Add to this the distraction of thinking about the departure and very quickly there is a situation in which a check can be missed. If there are concerns about the departure runway there is always the option of using the reciprocal after inspecting the runway surface, slope and departure wind. As the reporter in the following report notes, "There is never a legal requirement to use a particular runway". One of the contributory factors that could have been avoided was the long flat approach. Motor glider pilots can readily integrate into a powered approach circuit by conducting level-to-glide approaches. Many pilots of powered aircraft will also do this to practise glide approaches. Finally, when it comes to wheels-up landings there is an old saying: 'there are those pilots who have – and those who nearly have!' Being meticulous about a 'last chance' check on final approach will keep you in the second category.

NOTES:

YOUNG AND FUELLISH

CASA

Name withheld by request, Jul 12, 2017

It had been a picture perfect day when I set off from Brisbane on a solo NAVEX out west in a Cessna 206. After making it out to Moonie oil fields, I was returning via Warwick with a little under half tanks of fuel when I noticed a thick band of clouds over the ranges. After trying to make it over the top but being unsure of a gap to get back through, I set out to fly underneath. Soon I was crawling underneath the clouds and weaving through the ranges, with a few turnarounds required due to dwindling visibility. I decided to track south where it appeared to be clearer. There I ended up squeezing through a gap in the cloud to make it out over Casino.

I overflew Casino, noting that my fuel was getting quite low due to the time spent flying in circles trying to make my way over the ranges. I began monitoring it closely, glad I had kept an accurate fuel log for the initial part of the flight. However, the cloud was even thicker as I tried flying north towards Kyogle, and after checking NAIPS I noticed the area forecast (ARFOR) forecasting deteriorating conditions coming in from the east. A quick look at the radar on the Bureau of Meteorology site showed a band of showers stretching from south of Ballina to just north of Brisbane. I decided to land at Casino and formulate a plan of attack. Refuelling at Lismore was not an option as it was still under water from the floods the week before, so I had to conserve as much fuel as possible to return to Brisbane.

After calling my flight school for some extra advice, I decided to wait out the poor weather in Casino, then continue up along the coast once the showers to the east had moved past.

After an hour and a half of replanning and submitting a new flight plan to enter Gold Coast airspace, I dipped my tanks and set off again, well aware of the necessity to reduce fuel consumption as much as possible due to the tanks now reading a quarter full.

I tracked east and contacted Brisbane Centre for a code and clearance; however, due to the weather they were having difficulty identifying me, and as I flew low level through Nimbin TV towers, the terrain shielding prevented continuous communication. Coming out towards the east, the weather was not much better, but after obtaining a clearance, I was able to track via the western VFR route up to Brisbane, where the weather began to clear. Looking back on it, I can now see how close I was to busting VMC, and realise how much safer it would have been to request special VFR approaching the TV towers.

After landing, I dipped the tanks and noticed that I had landed with 50 litres remaining. Uh oh. With the 206 burning 60 litres/hour, that meant I had been five minutes off needing to declare an emergency. In my initial fuel plan, I had not subtracted the 45 minute fixed reserve, and was therefore planning on burning all fuel in the tanks, including the unusable reserves. This was a massive wake-up call to me, as in flight I hadn't even considered the requirement to make an emergency call due to fuel starvation, and would have blithely gone on to break the law by landing with less than 45 minutes remaining. It highlighted the importance of subtracting the fixed reserve from the initial fuel plan, as I would have been much more aware of how close I was entering emergency territory.

This incident didn't contain any engine failures, gear failures or unexpected parts flying off mid-flight, but it could have been a very real emergency if I hadn't pushed through marginal conditions and, luckily, landed with the remaining fuel I had on board.

An inaccurate fuel log and an extra five minutes of flying would have meant a whole world of paperwork, not to mention the inconvenience to ATC trying to direct a pre-CPL pilot who had inadvertently flown into fuel starvation to the nearest airport to refuel.

Keeping an accurate fuel log is crucial. You never know when you might need an extra few litres, especially on the coast where the ARFOR can go from perfect to poor in the space of three hours. Also, never be afraid to ask for help.

Instructors are there for a reason and my instructor provided well-needed, clear-headed advice to a very stressed pilot.

NOTES:

MORE THAN A TROPICAL BREEZE
CASA

by Jason MacLeod, May 10, 2017

In June 2016, I travelled to Bali for work but managed to make that coincide with a paragliding tour. With a newly minted licence and only 5.5 hours airtime, I was keen to get as much flying done as possible. Most of the flying happens in Candidasa, a challenging site on an old peanut farm. The launch involves leaping off terraces and contains all sorts of spiky, wing-destroying sappy trees. About five days into the trip, I launched on a particularly strong day. Two instructors assisted due to the strong winds. I relied too much on them. Propelled by my own eagerness, all I could think about was getting into the sky, pushing away my doubts about the conditions. I really shouldn't have launched. When I watch the video of my flight, the wind was barrelling up the hill and I was an inexperienced pilot on an A wing. After my crash, no-one else flew that day.

A video of the launch shows me going straight up even before I can turn around. All I remember was 'right brake, right brake' then my instructor yelling out 'speed bar'. Unfortunately I couldn't reach it in time. I was being thrown around in my harness and the bar was up high, tucked in its Velcro strap. By the time I had gone on bar I was just above the hill. As I pushed the speed bar out I dropped down below the hill. By that time I was in serious trouble. I started to turn away but too late. Rotor. I don't remember much but my vario shows me coming down about nine metres/second, straight into a cactus and rusty barbed-wire fence. My airbag cushioned much of the fall. Remarkably, I just missed three nasty strands of rebar sticking out of a concrete fence post. My only injuries were a few puncture wounds, cactus thorns and shock, but it could have been a lot, lot, worse.

My instructor and fellow pilots on the tour were quick to come to my aid. I think Marcus was the first on the scene. He told me to lie still and not move. Second, he unclipped my wing which was great because I was worried about being dragged through the barbed-wire fence. Be like Marcus to another pilot who crashes and you could make a big difference.

Glenn, a nurse, was also there soon afterwards. He checked for broken bones, concussion, treated my cuts from the barbed wire and helped me deal with the initial shock. Now I have promised myself to fly with a first-aid kit and keep my first-aid skills up. My instructor packed up my glider which was a big relief. I think one of the first things I asked was if my glider was OK. Crazy I know but such is the pull of our sport.

When I did get on my feet and back to the hill a few other pilots sat with me. That made a big difference. I remember Kieran not saying much but checking I was OK. I was still a bit shaken up, a bit sore and didn't want to talk, but having people around was great. It was only when I recomposed myself about an hour or so later that I was ready to take in what happened. Andrew, Glenn and Maderson all helped me understand what happened. We reviewed what they saw and I started to take note of the lessons I needed to observe.

A big one for me is a profound respect for rotor and strong winds. Going over the back was like being dumped in the surf—being drilled into the hard ground by a strong and powerful wave of turbulent air.

I also made a number of simple errors. In strong winds I need to recheck my speed bar. Now I have a little ditty I say to myself at the start of each flight, 'Holy Hell, Spandau Ballet', which refers to harness, helmet, speed bar. I need to always unclip my speed bar on launch in strong winds so it hangs down a bit. Then there are other basics. It is essential to assess my capabilities, review the site, check my flight plan and observe the conditions.

I don't feel any shame in crashing. For me the most important thing is that I learn from it. Flying is also an inner journey. I am grateful for the crash in that it made space for me to face fear full on and also accept again how dangerous the sport can be if we are not vigilant.

Getting up in the air as soon as possible was so important for me. Having experienced pilots and the paragliding community I was with, support that was a beautiful thing.

NOTES:

ACCIDENT REPORT

CHIRP

May 2017, Issue 72

Earlier this year I had the shame of my first flying accident and I can blame nobody but myself. I went for a short flight in my group's [aircraft type] from the strip where it has been based [for several years]. The weather was excellent and CAVOK all the way with about 3-4 OKTAS cloud cover. The flight went very well right up to the very last minute.

I had the strip in sight and called on [frequency] to announce arrival then again on downwind. Turned base and lined up with the runway, no crosswind at all. Time was very early afternoon so no sun in eyes problem, called final and made a perfect approach and only just as I flared and the mains were touching did I think, "where have all these weeds come from?" The ground was very rough and there was a bang underneath. The nose dropped, prop struck and left wing dropped.

"I have crashed and am unhurt" were my first thoughts followed by an immediate switching off of master switch and a hasty exit.

Looking at the scene I then realised I had chosen to land on the rough uncultivated strip alongside the runway which has a surface worse than a ploughed field.

What led me to identify this as the runway escapes me since I knew it was there. Being somewhat yellow in colour it is more evident than the runway, which is green, and the field alongside the runway on the other side was also green with new crop. However my brain had locked in to a decision and my concentration was on the technicalities of making another smooth landing. I have subsequently been told that this type of error is not unknown and even has a fancy name, confirmation bias.

Fortunately I have not damaged the structure and 2 new undercarriage legs and a new prop should fix it according to the experts. I do not expect to repeat this error but relate this story as a warning to others that what you believe you are doing may not actually be the real situation. Maybe I had relaxed my positional awareness because I "knew" the home field so well.

There were no runway markers on the airfield at the time of the incident but there are now which will serve to assist others not to repeat my error.

CHIRP Comment: This type of accident has happened in other places. Fortunately on this occasion the pilot was uninjured and the aircraft repairable. It is worth pointing out that, in addition to obvious damage, whenever a propeller is damaged by contact with the ground, vegetation etc. the engine should be checked for shock loading. The absence of runway markers was almost certainly a contributory factor in the incident but the reporter is correct to highlight confirmation bias as the probable cause:

Confirmation bias describes a situation where a person will ignore facts or information that does not conform to their preconceived mental model, and will assume as true any information that does conform to their beliefs (Nickerson, 1998).

This is very dangerous in all manner of ways in aviation and we are grateful to the reporter for bringing us this example of the phenomenon. Guarding against it is difficult but awareness is a good first step. Always be on your guard and if any single thing looks out of place, seems a bit odd or if you are doing something you have done many times before – beware!

NOTES:

NO PLACE FOR FUELING

CALLBACK

Mar 2017, Issue 446

[I] began to experience engine roughness followed quickly by a complete loss of power. I had already closed the IFR flight plan and was inbound to land. The engine lost power at 1,500 feet AGL, about 4 miles from [the airport] with 18 knots of headwind. Given the proximity to the ground and distance to the runway, [I] reversed course and began searching for a place to land. Seeing there was no immediate traffic on the highway, I decided to land [there], and the landing proceeded without incident.

Upon inspection of the aircraft, the cause was discovered for my loss of power. It was fuel starvation. The fuel selector switch had been set to the right tank, and the previous flight had been conducted while on only one tank. The chain of events...was set in motion by the complacency of the Pilot in Command (PIC) and failure to properly abide by checklist procedures in the cockpit. Familiarity with the aircraft led to a level of complacency on my part [with] the fuel selector switch and checklist flow during preflight. My belief that the selector switch was always on BOTH allowed the checklist item to go unnoticed. The flight [was] conducted with the aid of the autopilot, which prevented me from noticing the aircraft flying more and more out of trim while one [fuel] tank was being exhausted. Approaching the airport and disconnecting the autopilot, [I] noticed the trim situation, which was promptly overshadowed as the engine lost power. Ground proximity, aircraft configuration, airspeed, and the urgency of the situation prevented me from attempting corrective measures that might have restored engine power.

NOTES:

NO PLACE FOR DUELING COMPLACENCY

CALLBACK

Mar 2017, Issue 446

The Ground Controller advised me that an aircraft had taxied out and taken a wrong turn and that an aircraft would be holding short of the runway, waiting to cross. At that time a Bonanza advised me that he was holding short of the runway, ready for departure. I advised Ground Control that the aircraft that taxied the wrong way could wait until the Bonanza departed. I had a Cessna that was on short final for a touch and go. Once I had sufficient spacing, [I issued], "Bonanza, Runway 3, cleared for takeoff."

The Bonanza read back the runway and "Cleared for takeoff."

During this time of day, the sun was setting to the southwest, and we had the double shades pulled, making it difficult to see the approach end of the runway. My attention was focused to the approach end of the runway, looking for the Bonanza to depart, when I noticed an aircraft pass the tower departing the opposite direction runway [Runway 21].

I felt that complacency on my part was to blame. I should have observed the Bonanza at the approach end of the runway instead of taking his word for it. The pilot couldn't read a compass, read a runway sign depicting which way the runway goes, or familiarise himself with an airfield layout. This is a situation that I will probably never see again.

NOTES:

FORCED LANDING
CHIRP

Feb 2017, Issue 71

I was flying with my neighbour on a sight-seeing trip. I had fuelled the aircraft and had 9 gallons of fuel indicated. The flight was planned to last 1hr 15mins. On our return to the airfield I noted that I had 3 gallons indicated with 20 NM to run. As I made a joining call some 10 NM W of the field I looked again and noted 3 gallons still remaining. At that point the aircraft was at 1500′ AGL and was positioned for an overhead join. Abruptly the engine stopped. No coughing or temporary restoration of power. I entered a 50 kt glide, selected carb heat, switched between the main and aux tank (noting the gauge was showing 1 gallon remaining) and identified a suitable field. I had numerous options. Selecting the best, I declared a PAN with the local military zone controller and then continued with my emergency shutdown drill, reminding my passenger to tighten his harness. He was extremely calm and remained so as I made an into wind landing on a recently cropped field. The aircraft came to a halt within 100m with the propeller having stopped just on touchdown. I turned off all switches and we exited the aircraft. I then called the military zone controller to confirm we were safe and on the ground.

Lessons Learned:

I trusted my old gauge when I should have taken more fuel before the flight. I should have trusted my instincts and not believed we had 3 gallons left for such a long period of flight. I benefitted from being well versed in flying PFLs in the local area and converted my practice into a real approach and made a safe landing in a farm field.

CHIRP Comment: The reporter has correctly identified his mistake in trusting the fuel gauge. In many GA aircraft, particularly older types, dipping the tanks before flight is the only way to be confident about an aircraft's fuel state. That said, the reporter is commended for his cool head and presence of mind in carrying out a near text-book forced landing. A Mayday call would have been more appropriate than Pan, but the important point was to alert ATC and that was done successfully without compromising the priority task – flying the aircraft. Well done!

NOTES:

IN SICKNESS AND IN HEALTH
CASA

by Deborah Blackman and staff writers, Sep 14, 2016

My partner's and my four-year dream was about to come to fruition—we were departing on a 78-day flight from Brisbane through northern, central and Western Australia. In the excitement of it all little did I know that I would soon have a front-row, right-hand seat in a real-life emergency.

This is a story with important lessons for pilots and partners of pilots. I met my partner two years before this event, and, after a lengthy friendship, we became a couple. Almost straight away, I discovered his passion for flying, which was challenging, and exciting, but most of all scary to me.

My perception of light aircraft was an all-too-common one—'aren't they dangerous?' I wondered how I would react when he invited me to go flying with him. Being the type of person who wants to know all the ins and outs, I was interested in his quest and all the things that went into flying. It placed a whole new dimension on our relationship as I came to understand that his psyche, quiet demeanour, motivation, and attitudes were reflected in his role as a pilot. He's an individual who places extreme importance on maintaining a strong focus on healthy diet and high physical fitness levels.

The privileges of holding a Class II medical licence, a PPL and NVFR for a number of single-engine type aircraft are so important to him. When the opportunity came to go flying, I accepted the invitation with some trepidation. At the airport he checked the plane thoroughly, gave a safety brief, then asked me to hold a book/manual in a binder and proceeded to read aloud from the pages and do things with switches, dials etc.

'Oh my goodness,' I thought, 'he's reading out of a book, learning as he goes!' Then, after seemingly a long time and so many checks, again from this manual, he asked me, 'Are you OK to go? We are about to line up for take-off and if you don't want to go, please say so now, that's OK.'

At work the next week, I told all my colleagues about how scary it was, his reading out of a manual. Patiently, he took me through a whole lot of detail in plain simple English as the joy flight across Brisbane, out over the bay and back to Archerfield proceeded. On landing it was so smooth and gentle. Almost straight away we went flying again, both locally and long distance.

My confidence in him increased exponentially over this time as I sat next to him travelling in these small aircraft. I also enjoyed the privilege of flying with him on a couple of Angel Flights, and saw first hand what this meant to him. We planned an outback trip through Queensland and northern Australia, which was to be the holiday of a lifetime. As our tour time neared I watched, questioned and enjoyed immensely participating in the trip preparation. As he went over all probabilities again and again, I never imagined that anything could spoil this dream holiday.

A beautiful day dawned. The aircraft was packed and pre-flighted, with the paper work and all last-minute checks completed. The time had finally arrived! 'Good to go captain,' I said as we departed. We climbed, headed west, and made a couple of stops on the way to fuel and drop in on an old family friend. We had clear skies and fair winds, with a fabulous view of western Queensland.

The camera kept rolling. All was going to plan. I could see first hand the value of all the planning, and as we flew west, my partner would explain in basic terms what was happening: navigation, communications, controlling the plane on descents, joining the circuit and other things that made all this a reality. He had me directly involved in many facets of the flight, although I did have occasional trouble sighting the airfield and determining which way the windsock was blowing.

On the fifth day, we awoke to another beautiful clear, but somewhat windy, day. Departure was earlier than expected, so we had to rush to breakfast, get to the airport and start the long track north to get us to the Gulf by late afternoon, our next overnight stay.

The plan was to land and refuel about a third of the way there to ensure that the fuel margin was still good on arrival at our destination. On arrival, the windsock was flapping all over the place and sometimes was nearly horizontal. With very pronounced wind-gusts as we were about to land, a sudden and major change forced a go-around.

The second landing was successful and we taxied to re-fuel. Then my partner said, 'I don't feel well in the tummy.' After a lengthy conversation, it was decided we would depart with an alternative stop planned if the queasiness didn't abate. I felt a little uneasy, but on take-off everything seemed normal and we climbed into a beautiful blue sky.

Some 20 minutes after take-off, at 4500 feet, my partner said suddenly, 'I am feeling very ill, need to get down urgently, we are going back.' He became physically sick and turned the plane around to head back to where we had re-fuelled. He began to perspire profusely, was dry retching and become very pale. I watched in horror as his condition deteriorated and listened as he made a number of seemingly incoherent statements about actions, asking questions—sometimes repetitively— about heights, airport elevation and some instrument settings. I questioned him as to why he didn't land down there on that road and received short stilted answers.

We flew on, and as unobtrusively as I could, I reached for my mobile phone to text the kids to tell them we were in trouble and that I loved them. Suddenly we began descending, but I couldn't see the airport anywhere. Again the questions began: 'Do I have the airport in sight? What elevation is it? Can you see the windsock? Which way is it blowing? Keep an eye out for traffic.'

I finally saw the airport, but there seemed to be no pattern to our approach and he was asking me to 'be quiet, just answer questions'. I was having information overload and was frightened, but trying to stay calm.

Turning onto a long final, he was hunched forward with his stomach cramping, sweating even more, very pale and absolutely fixated by the grip on the control yoke. Down and down we went as on so many other landings before, but I wondered if we would make it. I was still frightened and hadn't sent any text messages. Was it too late? The landing in blustery conditions was bumpy, but quite good given the situation. I didn't care, only that we were safe.

The plane was taxied, shut down and secured. My partner staggered around and leaned against the cowling absolutely exhausted; mentally and physically drained.

On arrival at the local hospital the locum on duty (a part-time DAME) immediately ran a host of tests and my partner was effectively and rightfully grounded. With the help of prescription drugs and saline drips his body recuperated and he became his normal self again.

The tour was over and we returned to Brisbane on a commercial flight. Extensive medical tests by a range of specialists concluded that this was a one-off episode. The dream might have been badly interrupted, but most importantly, we kept our lives thanks to the skill of the pilot. He, under severe distress, applied the lesson: in emergencies—aviate, navigate and communicate. I subsequently went flying on a few trial instructional and partners-of-pilot type flights and regained every confidence I had before and went on to enjoy so many more uneventful flights with the man who has now become my husband.

Important lessons I would pass onto partners of general aviation pilots are to: involve yourself in all that they are doing to learn how it all works; if your partner's flying school offers one day courses, enrol and do it; and consider before each flight whether your partner is 'fit to fly'. And most importantly: trust your instincts. I wish I had been more assertive the first time about staying on the ground, so that the dream of a lifetime didn't become a near disaster.

NOTES:

HOT AND HIGH

CASA

Name withheld by request, Nov 12, 2015

As a fresh PPL pilot, I was always thrilled when I got to navigate across the state all by myself. The sense of achievement I got from sitting in an aluminium tube that hurtles through the sky at 200km/h, and somehow ends up at a predetermined location because of your inputs, was what fascinated me about flying. It was during February when I started my navigation flights to build hours towards my commercial pilot's licence. Flying from a school based in Melbourne, this meant generally excellent weather and lots of new places to explore.

On one particular Saturday in February, I had a solo cross-country flight booked in a Cessna 172. The day before the flight, I had put a lot of effort into creating a thorough flight plan to make things easier for me on the flying day. My route would take me up the Kilmore Gap to clear Melbourne control space, then head north west to land at St Arnaud, followed by Echuca for another landing, finally coming back down south to return to my flying school. Looking at the area forecast on the day, there was nil significant weather until about

4pm, when large cumulonimbus would be building. Not to worry, I should be home by 3pm. Although much to my dislike, the mercury was tipped to reach 43 degrees at 2pm. Wow, what a stinker!

I departed at about 10:30am, and the first segment to St Arnaud was uneventful, albeit a bit hot and bumpy. After completing a few touch and goes, I departed overhead towards my next landing point at Echuca. It was at this time that I wished I had eaten more before I left, as my stomach was starting to give me grief. The hot and bumpy conditions only made things worse. Then I realised that the aircraft I was flying was fitted with air conditioning; an aftermarket feature designed for a sick pilot like me, flying in 43 degree heat, who was in desperate need of some relief. I'd never used the air con before, but hey, how hard could it be? 'High' or 'low', 'on' or 'off'? *'I'll take 'high' and 'on' please Mr. Cessna,'* I said to myself. Soon I was cool as a cucumber, and happily on my way to Echuca.

It wasn't long before I had forgotten about the aircon, as I focused my attention on preparing for my arrival at Echuca. I joined crosswind for runway 36, and started the before-landing checks. I had always been told to complete these checks without using the paper checklist, as eyes must stay outside in the circuit. As far as I was aware, the 'A' in BOUMFAH only stood for 'autopilot disengaged'. I was soon to be proven very wrong.

As I descended on base, something felt different from normal. I couldn't quite figure out what it was, so I checked all my engine gauges and instruments. Everything looked normal and I continued the approach. As I turned final, there was a large updraft of warm air that caused me to become high and fast on approach. In response to this, I reduced power to idle, extended full flap, and held my aim point.

At about 400 ft, I glanced down at the tachometer, and was surprised to see a reading of about 350 rpm. The normal reading is about 1500 rpm. A few seconds later, at what I think was about 300 ft, the engine and propeller stopped dead. I can't recall exactly what happened after this point, but the next thing I can remember was touching down on the grass area just past the perimeter fence, and rolling onto the sealed runway.

'WHAT HAD JUST HAPPENED,' I THOUGHT. 'WAS THAT AN ENGINE FAILURE? I THINK IT WAS. WHAT DO I DO NOW? MAYBE YOU SHOULD TRY THE ENGINE FAILURE CHECKS? YES, I'LL TRY THAT.'

I sat on the runway for about two minutes, trying to restart the engine. But every time I turned the magnetos to start positions, the propeller hardly moved. Then I realised that there was something violently shaking the rudder pedals. 'What could that be? Let's get out and see what the heck is happening.' As I climbed out, it became obvious that the violent shaking of the rudder pedals was actually my legs shivering as a result of shock. I pushed the aircraft about 200 metres to the nearest taxiway to clear the runway; this was extremely difficult with shaking legs and 43 degree heat. I figured I was in need of food and a drink. I got a taxi into town and purchased lunch.

Upon returning to the airport, I finally built up the courage to get back in the aircraft and try to figure out what was wrong. It wasn't long before I realised that every time I turned on the master switch to try and start the engine, I could hear blaring fans from behind the glare shield, and feel air being blown onto my face. This explained the unusual feeling I had on base, and why I couldn't start the engine on the ground. The aircon was still switched on. As it turned out to me, the 'A' in the before landing checklist was also marked as 'Air conditioning—off/not applicable', although this was not listed as a read back item, so I had never actually used it before. After finally starting up, I completed three sets of run-ups, not finding any problems with the engine, taxied to the runway for my delayed return home.

On the way home, I entered the flight plan into the GPS and turned on autopilot. I had had enough navigating for that day.

Unfortunately, like a final curse from the gods of aviation, I encountered severe turbulence from building cumulonimbus on the way home. My late departure from Echuca had caused me to encounter the forecast storms developing on the way home. The result of this was my lunch making an unscheduled exit through my mouth just before landing back at home. Finally, I touched down; I had never been happier to be home.

On the following Monday, I submitted an incident report and discussed the events with the chief instructor. He believed the engine stoppage could have been caused by the air conditioning taking power away from the engine. As I had reduced power to idle on short final, the rpm had dropped to such a slow speed that the engine simply stopped. I believe that due to the conditions on the day, a very high-density altitude meant the engine's power output was already significantly reduced. This combined with low idle speed and the aircon belt taking power away from the crankshaft, was enough to cause engine failure.

It haunts me to think what the outcome might have been had I been on a runway with trees on the approach, or lost power just a few seconds earlier than had happened. Nowadays, I always check for Air Conditioning OFF before any landing, and more importantly, I give the checklists' a lot more respect. I love flying, and I hope to make it a safe career for myself. Hopefully my story will cause others to learn from my mistake, and maybe even save a life.

NOTES:

RUNNING OUT OF FUEL

CHIRP

Nov 2015, Issue 66

The day's planned flight from [ ] to [ ] to land, have lunch and fly back. 65 nautical miles each way, the aircraft uses about 10 litres per hour and cruises between 60 – 70 kts. I have done this sortie before in this aircraft. Flight time of about 1 hour in each direction, flying wind was a 10 kt northerly so a tail wind for the outbound and a headwind for the homebound leg. The aircraft has a sight tube on the cockpit rear bulkhead to show the fuel state. On DI the sight tube was showing 27 litres, the fuel capacity is 30 litres. I decided not to fill the tank as my expected fuel use was about 20 litres. The outbound flight was uneventful although more fuel had been used than expected. There was still showing sufficient for the return even at a higher usage rate. The homebound flight routed close to several airfields that could have provided fuel but the indicated fuel state during the flight appeared fine. When we were abeam [ ] with 20km to run it still showed 8 litres, this should have been plenty. When I reported at the southern VRP at 1000' the engine stopped and the sight tube showed no fuel. It became obvious that we would not make the airfield so I landed in a farmer's field - 2 fields short. The aircraft was undamaged and there was no other damage caused.

Lessons Learned:

Sight tube fuel gauges are not accurate and should not be trusted especially below 10 litres. The only reliable way to measure the fuel economy is to fill the tank to the brim, fly for an hour and fill it again.

Fuel usage should be checked at least annually to confirm it has not changed.

CHIRP Comment: The runway behind you; the sky above you; fuel in the bowser...... We are grateful to everyone who reports to CHIRP for sharing their experiences. Sight tubes can be more accurate than gauges but they require calibration; they are not accurate if the aircraft attitude in flight or on the ground is different from the calibrated position. The calibration, usually done by adding known quantities of fuel to an empty tank, also needs to take into account the amount of fuel that is unusable at the bottom of the tank. Finally, sight tubes can be difficult to read accurately in flight in turbulence and if they are not positioned where they can be easily seen by the seated pilot. The reporter's suggestion of checking the fuel usage periodically is a good one but actual usage can be significantly different from any controlled test. The weight of the pilot, passengers and luggage are variables and even minor variations in speed, trim and fuel/air mixture can have cumulative and significant effects. Having taken all of these factors into account and produced a fuel plan, it is important to allow a margin. There is little pleasure in returning to base 'on fumes' so in similar circumstances in the future it would be better to set off with full tanks and, having reached the outbound destination, make a realistic reappraisal of the fuel plan for the return.

NOTES:

COMPLACENCY OR PARANOIA?

CASA

by Charles Day, Mar 16, 2015

Last season I performed my first wheel-up landing (with no damage fortunately), so perhaps it's a sign that my razor-sharp concentration is starting to fade?

This gliding season there were perhaps further indications of geriatric deterioration. I was caught out twice in similar circumstances when gambling with the weather. The first time, there was a trough line running north–south to the west of Benalla, slowly advancing eastwards, heavy cirrus and a strong north wind ahead of it, a westerly behind, but some good cumulus to the north. The only chance of a cross-country flight was to chase the cumulus north to Lake Urana, then return just before the trough killed all convection near Benalla. I left my arrival too late and my finals turn onto runway 35 coincided with an instantaneous, gusty wind shift to the west. Somehow the 90-degree crosswind landing was achieved without damage.

The second episode, late in February, was even more dramatic. The forecast was again for a north–south trough line well to the west of Benalla, slowly advancing east, but this time with embedded cumulonimbus, rain squalls and lightning. The wind was a strong northerly ahead of the trough. There seemed to be plenty of time to have a similar flight north to about Oaklands, then get back on the ground at Benalla before the fireworks. By the time I got back to Yarrawonga, about 60km out, the trough was looking fairly evil, with curtains of rain and sporadic lightning not too far west of Benalla. The GPS drift while circling revealed that the northerly wind had increased considerably. Fortunately, I had plenty of height above glide slope and continuous weak lift ahead of the trough gave even more.

Approaching Benalla, I estimated that I would be able to land about 10 minutes ahead of the rain and squalls, which at that time were about 10km to the west, so I entered a close-in circuit for runway 35 with excess height. The water ballast was kept on board to provide extra gust-penetrating momentum. On downwind leg, which was extremely turbulent, I glanced west over Benalla and noticed that the whole town was suddenly covered in dense dust, which was being whipped up by a ferocious northerly.

Clearly, extreme measures were called for in landing in such conditions. I turned finals very high, just outside the airfield boundary fence, left both landing and cruise flap settings at zero and approached steeply to make headway against the gale. The airspeed fluctuated uncontrollably between about 55 and 90 knots and the ground run was very short, finishing only about 300m inside the boundary fence. It was necessary to keep the canopy locked and stay strapped in. Dive brakes were kept out, stick forward, wheel brake applied and full negative flap selected to reduce the chance of the aircraft being blown over. Rain started after a few minutes, accompanied by a violent wind shift to the west that swung the aircraft ninety degrees (despite the non-castoring tail wheel).

Ten minutes later, the rain passed and the wind dropped. Bob and Nick had judged things a lot better, landing about ten minutes ahead of me and missing much of the drama. Later, people on the ground estimated the squall at having been at least fifty knots! Substantial branches were stripped from trees.

Only a week later, and still twitching from this episode, I resolved to increase my margins and not push my luck with the weather again. The forecast was for a light southerly, with large cumulus and extensive showers developing later in the day near Benalla and the adjacent hills—but no lightning. The best option was for a triangular flight to the west and to gamble on getting high enough on the final leg for a long final glide into Benalla, dodging the showers. I accordingly declared a conservative triangle of about 535km to Boort, Maryborough and back to Benalla. If all went to plan, I would be home before things got dramatic.

The flight was initially slow, with a low cloud base, then much better under fairly good cumulus. I arrived at Maryborough at about 4 pm, full of confidence. Heading homewards, the direct track to Benalla passed about 20km south of Bendigo, then over Lake Eppalock, but that soon proved impossible, with a huge storm blocking the way and solid murk further south of track. Running northeast along the western edge of the rain gave off-the-clock lift to 6500 ft at 100 kt for a fair distance, but after that there was only a small patch of sunlight visible towards Benalla. With 160km to go and solid blackness ahead my confidence slumped. Benalla CTAF frequency was ominously silent. My options were closing in.

The best bet seemed to be to keep on track while I was still high, to see if any convection developed under the overcast, but it soon became clear that a stream of cold air was flowing north up the Goulburn Valley from the Kilmore Gap towards Shepparton and cutting off all potential thermals at the socks. A bold diversion further north was called for, where there was still sunshine and the remnants of the earlier good conditions. I ended up just west of Kyabram, 50km north of the direct track to Benalla. At least Shepparton airfield was clear and within range if the next storm, which was north of the town, produced no lift. With the memory of the traumatic landings at Benalla near storms fresh in my mind, I was a bit paranoid, and determined to land at an airfield with a windsock, come what may. An out-landing in a paddock could easily end up tangling with a strong wind from any direction, due to low-level outflows from storms.

Fortunately, the Shepparton storm elevated me back to near cloud base. I then had marginal final glide height to get to Benalla, barring no extensive sink under the complete overcast and widespread showers—not a good bet! Plan A was to hope for something brewing up on the way to give a decent glide margin. Plan B was to lob into the Dookie Agricultural College airstrip almost half way to Benalla if things went bad. Plan C was to turn back to Shepparton airfield. In the event, I got a weak climb to a safe height near Dookie and a light aircraft over Benalla assured me that there was a clear path between the heavy showers to get through. I landed without incident at almost 7 pm much later than planned. There had been no gliding at Benalla since about 4 pm, on account of continuous overcast and periodic rain.

Who knows if this season's lessons will linger in the remaining grey matter until next summer?

NOTES:

READING ON A TRAIN SAVED MY LIFE

CASA

Name withheld by request, May 10, 2014

In 1999, I was about two thirds of the way through my aviation degree in Melbourne, which incorporated the usual flying components all the way through to CPL and either an instructor rating or instrument rating.

Fresh out of high school and straight into university, I attacked the program with everything I had and achieved my PPL, as well as my night VFR.

It was the evening after the Phillip Island motorcycle grand prix. My cousin had hitched a ride down to the track from Melbourne. Shortly after the race, I received a call from him asking if I could fly down and pick him up. He couldn't organise a return trip from the island, and I was his last resort.

This would be my first night flight solo.

I remember telling my cousin that I wouldn't get there until after dark, and that I had plenty to organise beforehand, such as the 75 minute journey to Moorabbin airport. As is typical for a struggling student pilot, I had very little money to throw around and hence no car. Home alone that night, I offered a friend a free flight to Phillip Island and back, in return for a lift to the airport.

While waiting for my chauffeur, I checked the weather. It looked as though it was going to be tight ... fog was forecast to roll in over Phillip Island right when I was due there. I did my flight plan in the car. Adding to the time pressure was the fact that I wasn't night current and had to do three night circuits before I could pick up my friend, who was waiting in the flying school, and then depart for Phillip Island. Beginning to see a pattern? Time pressures and seemingly minor hurdles - all starting to line up.

Night circuits in Moorabbin gave me a false set of confidence - the surrounding city lights made it like flying in the day.

Anyone who has flown to Phillip Island at night might recall the airport being quite difficult to find, as the runway is relatively close to a small residential area, and their lights blend together; or maybe it was just me and my inexperience.

I flew along the southern coast of the island from west to east, and only when I saw the bridge to the mainland did I realise that I had missed the airport. After a 180 degree turn, the cockpit lit up brilliantly from the strobe lights, in what appeared to be descending fog. It only lasted a couple of seconds, but really got my nerves going. I had to hurry!

I landed without any major incident and picked up my cousin, who had been waiting there for hours. We taxied to the end of runway 18, for a take-off to the south.

The Phillip Island airport elevation is 43 feet. Once you pass the end of the runway, with an overcast sky, it is pretty much pitch blackness all the way to Tasmania. I remember lining up and consciously telling myself to get that T-scan going once I was airborne.

With everything checked and ready, I set take-off power and rolled down the runway. Rotating and setting the climb attitude, the world below quickly disappeared, and ahead it turned as black as black can be. Head down and onto the instruments I went. There I was T-scanning away, when on about a mid-upwind, in a moment of utter shock, I realised that the Piper Warrior's fixed-pitch prop was increasing rpm! In an instant, I knew what had happened.

I clearly remember my moment of clarification. I snapped my head around and saw the lights of the adjacent residential area at about the same level as the aircraft! I pulled back on the control column and reset climb attitude on the attitude indicator.

That was it.

The rest of the flight back to Moorabbin was uneventful.

After the flight, and over the years since, I have often wondered how close I came to spearing the three of us into Bass Strait. Quite possibly, that 43 feet elevation saved us, but then again, I could have been higher than I thought ... God only knows.

As soon as I heard the rpm increasing, I realised I had succumbed to the somatogravic illusion—I had let my inner ear rather than the attitude indicator steer the plane, and having done that, I had mistaken acceleration for pitch. As the aircraft accelerated, I interpreted it as the nose pitching up. I reacted by unconsciously lowering the nose slightly. As a result the aircraft accelerated. Again I interpreted this as pitch, and so on. Eventually, after a series of forward pitching, I was unknowingly descending into the blackness ahead.

I believe I picked up this illusion only because previous degree-related studies had fascinated me. One paper I read was about fighter pilots in World War II who were mysteriously crashing after night take-offs. Only then did we begin to understand these sensory problems.

The primary lesson I learnt is that we must actually read and understand our instruments, not just look at them in a predetermined sequence.

On top of this was the classic chain of events that could have led to an accident. The last link in that chain was broken back on a train ride to uni, when I read that WWII paper.

Fifteen years and 9000 hours later, I still do not take anything for granted. I will always wonder though—how close was I to meeting my maker?

NOTES:

TOO TIRED TO GLIDE

CASA

Mar 25, 2014

I had flown a Cessna 182, along with three friends, to a nearby glider field, so we could all have some gliding experience and enjoy the hospitality of the gliding club for a few hours. This wasn't the first time, so I was well versed about the extended time on the ground and the extra ground handling tasks while waiting for your turn to go flying. Gliding is a very labour-intensive exercise, and probably requires more patience than many people expect. However, I eventually got a couple of flights in, as did my friends.

The glider being used for training flights that day was the LET 13 Blanik, and the club had essentially given us sole use of the aircraft and one instructor for the day, as other flying was mainly being done in the single-seaters. For aero-towing duties, the club had an old Piper Tri Pacer, with barely enough power to launch the Blanik, but that only added to the training value of the exercise! With the Blanik and several single-seaters flying, the Tri Pacer was kept fairly busy for most of the day, only stopping for fuel and a brief rest at lunch for a BBQ.

My group had decided to finish by around 1600, in order to leave us time to fly home and put the 182 to bed by a civilised hour, so at the appointed time, with no further flights likely for the Blanik, it was decided that I would go along for the final 'hangar flight' and take some photos at the same time. Since I would not be flying it, and it would essentially be just a launch, fly past and landing, I wasn't even being charged for it. Win!

As we strapped in for the flight, Neville, the instructor, commented that it had been a great day, but he was glad this was the last flight because he was feeling quite fatigued. Essentially, he'd been in the seat all day, only getting out for lunch and a couple of toilet breaks. I gave it no further thought, although I too was suffering from the long day in the sun without enough water, so I knew how Neville felt.

The canopy was closed, towline hooked up, and wing-walker in place to launch, and off we went. I was happily snapping away with my Nikon, getting some quite good photos of the initial take-off run etc., so it only dawned on me rather late that we were taking much longer to get airborne and climb away this time. The tow plane had become airborne, then settled back to the ground shortly afterwards, seemingly with a power problem. However, it struggled skywards again, and managed to clear the boundary fence by about three metres, all the time with us hanging on behind just above his level as we also struggled to remain airborne. Clearly, something was amiss, but we had no real options available to get us back to the runway, so we stayed hooked up.

Eventually, the poor old Tri Pacer gave up the race, and I have a great photo of its main undercarriage splayed out at a rather flat angle as it bounced off the road alongside the airport perimeter. At the same time, the tow rope went slack as the tow pilot released us to climb away and circle back for a landing. We had almost nowhere to go, so quickly, Neville decided the road was the only place where we could reasonably land from this height and speed. He stood the poor old Blanik on its left wing in a desperate effort to line up with the road. By this time, the speed had washed off, and of course, the steep turn only made it worse, so we came crashing down onto the road, essentially wings level, but VERY hard.

After a very short landing roll, we came to a stop and Neville and I unstrapped and climbed out to push the glider off the road and away from traffic. Fortunately, there were no cars on the road when we 'landed' and none came along for the next 15 to 20 minutes.

While we waited for a couple of club members to bring a vehicle over and tow us back to the airfield, Neville and I were busy trying to work out just what had gone so horribly wrong. Obviously the tow plane had trouble getting us airborne and climbing away, so our initial thoughts were that he had some kind of engine problem, but he'd managed to get back to the runway after a normal circuit, so perhaps that wasn't the problem after all? Then, I saw that our spoilers were extended fully and commented to Neville that in the short time available he had done well to get them out for landing, but wouldn't flaps have been more useful? His response-that he hadn't deployed the spoilers at all-made us realise ... we now had the answer to the performance problem!

We discussed the spoilers for some time, but neither of us could remember seeing them extended before take off, so they must have been retracted, but the handle not properly latched. The take-off bumps and rattling had presumably moved the handle just enough to make the spoilers extend, and suddenly the tow plane had a much greater load to haul airborne. Given that it was a little marginal in power for towing the Blanik even under ideal conditions, the extended spoilers had caused enough drag to prevent climb. He had just enough power to get us to the scene of the accident ...

A simple mistake to make, and one he wouldn't normally have made I'm certain, if Neville hadn't been pretty much in the seat for five hours and clearly fatigued. We shouldn't have flown that last sortie-only saving the small effort of towing the Blanik back to the hangar behind a car. Instead, we had bent metal. It could have been much more serious if there had been traffic on the road, or any one of a number of other things had gone just a little differently. We had been very lucky to survive with no injury to anything except pride. However, the Blanik didn't fly for the next few months, while it was repaired.

Since then, there have been many times when my work day has been extended, or I haven't had enough rest the night before, and I've had cause to reflect on the insidious nature of fatigue. We often don't realise that we are even becoming fatigued until it's too late. Flight and duty time limitations are in place for a very good reason, but we can still become fatigued while working within those limitations, so they are only a guide anyway. Certainly, I've become much more aware of my own levels of performance degradation with increasing fatigue. In my case, it seems to begin with my radio calls becoming more sloppy and poorly planned. My next symptom is a general lack of maths ability, when even simple calculations of time intervals, or fuel remaining, take more effort. Of course, others' symptoms may be different, so all I can recommend is you watch for the insidious signs of fatigue and try to spot if your performance is degraded. If it is, you need to shorten your day, or get some rest. Know your symptoms and don't fly fatigued.

NOTES:

CHAPTER 3

HUMAN FACTORS & DECISION MAKING

"I've never seen an airplane yet that can read the type ratings on your pilot's license."

Chuck Boedecker

TRACK OF LANDING AIRCRAFT

CHIRP

Feb 2017, Issue 71

I was the pilot of an aircraft waiting at the hold to depart and noted an aircraft that wanted to use the hard runway to depart contrary to the grass runway that was in use.

Its pilot was advised that the runway in use was [ ], he insisted that he was going to use the hard runway. He then subsequently advised that he was going to take-off on r/w [ ] as he felt the wind favoured that runway. He was again advised that the grass runway was being used but he advised that he was exercising his pilot's discretion.

He took off across the track of landing aircraft which, in order to follow the airfield's circuit pattern for that runway, had to make an offset approach and would not have seen the departing aircraft. I felt that the actions of the [departing] pilot were very dangerous and could have led to a serious accident which, being near the ground, would have resulted in a number of fatalities. The airfield was very busy with an aircraft in the circuit and numerous aircraft landing and taking-off as the airfield operators would confirm if asked.

Lessons Learned:

As I was a pilot observing the actions of the [departing] pilot, I was horrified that a qualified pilot could consider such action and take such a risk. This is a case where the airfield ought to be able to instruct the pilot that he could not use the runway he wished to use in view of the danger to landing aircraft and if he continued against those instructions report him to the CAA.

CHIRP Comment: Please see the CHIRP comment for the next report.

NOTES:

TAKING-OFF

CHIRP

Feb 2017, Issue 71

I have a very embarrassing human factors admission to make which is entirely my fault – see below.

On the day of the incident, whilst the longest runway at our local (uncontrolled) airfield was the designated in-use runway, I elected to use an alternative (into wind) runway for my take-off. When ready for departure, the circuit was busy and another aircraft was almost ready to enter the main runway to take off. Rather than wait for it all to calm down and then take my turn, for some reason I decided to take off in between one aircraft landing and the next one, on the basis that I would only be crossing the active runway for a moment and could do this without impeding anyone else's activity. I called that I was taking-off from the minor runway, whereupon the pilot on final informed me that he was landing. I responded saying to the effect that it was OK as I had plenty of time to stay clear of him, and proceeded with my take-off which was uneventful and (as far as I am aware) so was the landing of the aircraft whose path I had crossed.

Although mathematically my reasoning was accurate (there was probably a good 15 seconds between our paths crossing), it was nonetheless unsound for several reasons:

1. It was a contravention of SERA.3210 (c) (4) (Right of way), which states that "An aircraft...shall give way to an aircraft landing or in the final stages of an approach to land".
2. One can imagine scenarios in which some form of failure during my take-off run could result in my coming to a halt at the intersection in front of the landing aircraft.
3. Even with everything working as expected, my action could have negatively distracted the landing pilot during the phase of flight in which we need a high level of concentration.

I have been flying for nearly 30 years, during which time I have avidly read "I learned about flying from that" reports, GASIL reports, CHIRP reports, and books about pilot error, and take safety very seriously. And yet I can still fall victim to impatience. I have a rule with flying and driving which I failed to follow this time – if you're rushing, wait. None of us can ever be too vigilant.

CHIRP Comment: This report does not refer to the same incident as the previous report. They occurred at different aerodromes but both places provide Air/Ground radio communications services. Although the reports speak for themselves – and we are grateful to both reporters – it is worth noting that Air/Ground operators can pass traffic and weather information but "Personnel providing an Air/Ground Communication Service must ensure that they do not pass a message which could be construed to be either an air traffic control instruction or an instruction issued by FISOs for specific situations." Aircraft commanders may elect to use any available runway provided that their aircraft movements can be safely integrated with other traffic.

NOTES:

C150 PILOT'S REPORT

CALLBACK

Oct 2016, Issue 441

Situation: My mission for the day was to fly to look at an airplane I was considering purchasing. Another pilot, who had a VFR only Cessna 150, [offered] his airplane for the flight. The weather was forecast to be marginal VFR with some IFR along the route [and] ceilings of 800 to 1,000 feet, becoming broken to clear as the day progressed. The weather was forecast to be bad the following day, so I "had" to take the flight that day. To complicate issues, I needed to... pick my son up from school that evening.

I was paying close attention to the weather en route.... A couple stations near our destination [were] reporting marginal VFR broken conditions, and an airport near the destination was VFR. It took me another hour to realise that the VFR airport report was 4 hours old and was not being updated by ADS-B. I had received a weather brief earlier that day, and I supplemented it with my iPad, but my weather program was not updating. I was still on the 4 hour old weather at our departure time.

This plane literally had no equipment. We had a handheld

transceiver and [a] portable, [ADS-B capable] GPS unit. We could get 5 miles of range out of the handheld on a good day. At least [we had] an attitude indicator. All the areas within range of our fuel supply were reporting anywhere from low IFR to 1,000 feet overcast ceilings and 5 miles visibility. We were now 2 hours into the flight, and I was waiting for the ADS-B to refresh.

What Would You Have Done?

The Reporter's Action:

▪ We continued another half hour... At this point, the left fuel gauge was bouncing off "E". We did find an airport at the very edge of our fuel supply that was reporting 1,000 foot broken ceilings, and [we] set course for it... I... [chose] an airport well away from a major city that was reporting good visibility below the clouds and (reasonably) high ceilings. I dialled up an RNAV approach on my handheld, switched to UNICOM (figuring I could break things off if I heard another plane on the approach), and into the soup we went. We broke out of the clouds right at 1,000 feet, landed safely, and had 3 gallons of fuel remaining... We waited a couple hours on the ground for conditions to improve, then continued to our destination. Lesson for the day: nothing, and I mean nothing, is worth taking a chance like that.

NOTES:

TAXIWAY INCIDENT

CHIRP

Aug 2016, Issue 69

Whilst taxiing for departure, undertaking checks DI, minor distraction resulted in departure from taxiway through adjacent pebble trough onto waterlogged grass. Prop struck by pebble, severity of which required replacement of prop.

While rounding the bend on the taxiway I was checking DI and compass per normal. I did not notice deviation of aircraft until the left main wheel slipped from taxiway into a trough of pebbles. This was about 18 inches wide running the length of the taxiway. Two attempts to turn right and leave the trough were unsuccessful due to the taxiway edge being above the level of pebbles. I therefore decided to turn left onto grass which I assessed as suitable to continue on and then return to the taxiway.

Unfortunately grass area was heavily waterlogged and within a second or two I was bogged down to axles. At that point, contact with tower advised to shut down and they would send fire crew to pull aircraft free. Once they arrived, an examination of prop showed severe damage to prop about 3 inches from tip, leading edge cut with semi-circular hole 2-3mm diameter. Fortunately the prop had not struck the ground.

After recovery, engineers inspected and confirmed severe damage. When engine run at full power, no vibration or other noise detected.

Comments from Tower and fire crew were that 'I was not the first or the last person to experience this type of incident' and there had been others at the airfield but no indication of similar damage.

What did I learn?

1. Compass and DI checks can easily be made without 'wiggling' aircraft – taxi turns will always be normal.
2. Always assess taxiway widths – some are narrower than others.
3. Always check taxiway surfaces and adjacent areas for potential hazards.
4. If unfortunate to leave normal route (taxi or runway) shutdown immediately – do not attempt to extricate with turn or power.

My experience shows that the [airfield] management have introduced a hazard without full assessment of risk. Having spoken to several pilot friends who use [the airfield], the pebble trough is not obvious to those taxiing (unless like me, they slip into it). The taxiway appeared in hindsight narrower than usual, although adequate. Any small distraction, causing an aircraft to deviate from centreline, takes it close enough to pick up a stone and prop strike. Whilst accepting [the] intention of drainage, the pebble trough should be covered with sufficient sand or earth to prevent stone pick up. It would be very useful if the Tower advised all pilots or those visiting of the potential hazard and to ensure careful taxiing along centreline or to right.

CHIRP Comment: Stone filled drainage ditches are common at airfields but they are often sprayed with a bitumen type material to bind the stones and minimise any FOD hazard. Instrument checks can be tricky in congested areas or on taxiways – if necessary they can be delayed until turning on to the runway. If an aircraft should stray off the paved surface onto an unprepared or hazardous area, the reporter is absolutely right – don't attempt to use power to extricate it; shut down and get assistance.

NOTES:

ALL FINGERS AND TOES

CASA

Jul 22, 2016

It was a crisp, early morning—cool enough to make your fingertips slightly numb, but a perfect flying day: no cloud and no wind. I had yet to gain my RA-Aus flying certificate, but was well on the way with four solo hours under my belt in the school's silver Sportstar. My regular instructor wasn't on duty that day, so it was the CFI, who had a rather odd disposition, in that he only seemed to be happy when he was either upset or angry about something or other—and this was most of the time.

We got on OK though. He was busy with another student pre-flighting the silver Sportstar, so I was to have the white one today—same plane but different set up—an early glass cockpit. I had flown this plane once or twice before, but was not completely comfortable with the different layout. There was also a problem adjusting the pedal position on this plane, as it lacked an operating lever. This meant it was a two-handed job to move the pedals to one of three positions. I had noted this on a previous flight and mentioned it to the instructor—the parts were 'coming'.

The CFI gave me a 'challenge' for the day's solo flight—an expanded flight envelope and circuit joining exercises. He went back to the other student and I got on with the pre-flight. Everything OK, time to adjust the pedals to the mid position, my normal flying set up. With head and shoulders in the foot well, I struggled for what seemed like ages to get the pedals to move, all to no avail. The numb fingers didn't help. I had to call for assistance—this made the CFI really happy and after he had just about blown a blood vessel getting the pedals adjusted, it was my plane. I pitied the other student—at least I was getting out of there.

I hopped in the plane, buckled up and found the pedals were in the wrong position—they were full back, forcing my knees backwards and up into an uncomfortable flexed position. What to do? Call the CFI again—no I didn't think that a good idea—he was happy enough after the last episode.

'It'll be OK,' I thought to myself—start motor and taxi—with some pedal brake inputs to get used to the new position. I was anxious to get on with the 'challenge'—nothing could go wrong on such a glorious day.

Make the calls, do the run-ups and thinking about the new 'challenge' the CFI gave me. Line up, smooth application of power and go! Some right rudder to keep her straight—50 metres into the take-off roll with full power and then veering violently to the left; no time to think, no time to react before hitting a wide, deep culvert to the left of, and parallel to, the runway.

Stunned but not hurt, engine off, electrics off, I got out. Extensive damage to the aircraft undercarriage, wing and prop. So, what happened? I really did not know. All this made the CFI really, really happy (not), but to be fair he was good about it. After the mess was cleaned up he took me back to the office for a stiff drink—only coffee unfortunately.

I couldn't think straight for a few days, there was paper work to fill out, and I still hadn't worked out what happened—whatever it was, it was very quick. My confidence was totally shredded. Would I ever fly again? I doubted it.

As the mental fog lifted over the next week there was only one plausible explanation.

During the take-off roll, as I increased pressure on the right pedal, I must have also activated the right foot brake—this was due to the abnormal angle that my foot made with the incorrectly placed rudder pedals. This would have resulted gross overcorrection with the left rudder—leading to the culvert.

This incident was a classic 'Swiss cheese' event. Numb fingers leading to inability to deal with a defective pedal mechanism, leading to a cranky CFI also misplacing the pedals, leading to me accepting an unsafe situation rather than shutting the engine down and getting out of the plane until the situation was rectified. After all I had a 'challenge' to confront and conquer. Little did I know just how big that challenge would turn out to be. In retrospect I am glad that the culvert was there—it stopped the plane from ploughing into nearby hangars, which would have been much more serious for all concerned and could have easily led to fatalities—a close call indeed.

I did get back to flying after a few weeks, but did a lot of dual time before my confidence returned.

I went on to gain the RA certificate, and more recently, the PPL. Nowadays, whenever I hear myself saying *'it will be all right'* there is a loud voice in a deep recess of my brain which yells out *'no it won't - fix it'*! I hope that voice never fades.

NOTES:

HELICOPTER HAZARD

CHIRP

May 2016, Issue 68

I was carrying out circuits at [ ] on the unlicensed runway when the controller put a helicopter on the hover square [about 500m from the upwind end of the runway]. I pointed out this area was below the climb out, I was told in no uncertain terms that the aircraft was on the ground (at this stage it was not) and it did not encroach on the climb out. Either way the helicopter was in position for two circuits and only touched down after my comment. This distracted the student, and when you consider any number of things that could have gone wrong: we could have had an engine failure or the helicopter needed to lift off for some reason. Is it normal aviation practice to take off over a hovering helicopter? I suppose I should have declined to touch and go?

CHIRP Comment: As the runway in use is unlicensed, responsibility for safe operations on and from it lies with the aircraft commander. That said, Commanders are always responsible for the safety of their aircraft and, if concerned about the proximity of the helicopter, it would have been prudent to go around.

NOTES:

LIGHT BULB MOMENT
CASA

by Peter McCarthy and staff writers, May 18, 2016

As a young pilot with about 170 hours total experience, I agreed to make a five-day trip carrying university students on a cost-sharing basis. There were six passengers in two PA-28 aircraft, one a retractable Archer. The other pilot, more experienced than me, had worked as a flight service officer. We agreed to take turns flying the two aircraft.

The evening of the second day found us in Wollongong, where the students partied late and were rowdy back in our shared motel room. I had a few drinks with them and then lay awake for much of the night listening to a strong gusty wind, and worrying about whether I had tied the aircraft down adequately. I thought about calling a taxi in the early hours to go and check, but it was a 20-minute journey each way. Next morning we were up at six and skipped breakfast to visit an underground coal mine. There I had my first and only experience of sniffing snuff, which the miners used because they could not take cigarettes underground.

The mine visit ran late and it was mid-afternoon when we got back to the airfield. To save time we agreed that the other pilot would prepare and lodge both flight plans while I inspected and signed off both aircraft. We were quickly in the air, and then I discovered that we could not get a clearance direct to Scone as planned, but had to fly past Sydney coastal, adding substantially to the flight time. It was unclear to me the exact route we would be taking, so I couldn't plot it on the chart or calculate the flight duration. It seemed we would struggle to make last light but the other pilot, on the chat frequency, reassured me that there was pilot activated lighting (PAL) at Scone if we needed it. This was my day in the slower aircraft so he pulled steadily ahead of me.

We passed a couple of landing opportunities in the lower Hunter Valley, but the Arrow was well ahead of me and its pilot encouraged me on. Although lights were already beginning to appear on the ground there was, reassuringly, bright daylight at altitude. When we arrived at Scone there was no PAL available and a combination of high ground and heavy cloud to the west made the airfield an inky shadow, though the town lights shone clearly. The other pilot, who unlike me had a night VMC rating, was still confident and handled communication with Flight Services for both of us. They arranged for some airfield employees to provide emergency lighting for our landing while we orbited the field. To do this they had to cut a padlock on the perimeter fence and line up two cars with crossed headlights on the threshold, with a third car at the other end of the runway for an aiming point. I turned on my landing light and made my first and only night landing without incident.

While filling in the incident report form, I thought deeply about what had gone wrong. I should have made sure the aircraft was securely tied down when I did it, and I was probably too fatigued to fly, but the real problem was that I had abrogated my responsibility for the flight entirely to the other pilot. I was somewhat in awe of his additional experience and knowledge and all too eager on that day to let someone else do all the thinking. While filling in my log book I wondered whether the two hours should go in the in-command column. I wasn't really in command of that flight.

NOTES:

GET THERE 'ITIS'
CASA

Name withheld by request, Sep 9, 2015

After having recently achieved my private pilot's licence, I decided to take up an offer from a friend to fly to the north-western Victorian town of St. Arnaud. My mate has a property there and upon my arrival he was to pick me up from the airport. I contacted him and organised to stay for a couple of days before flying back home again. That part of the planning was done. I booked an aircraft, a Cessna 172R, with my flying school at Moorabbin Airport. I then commenced my flight planning for the trip which I was hoping to undertake the following week, weather permitting. Being my first overnight exercise, I wanted everything to go to plan. My instructor always told me that the better prepared I was for the flight the less chance there was of things going wrong (eliminate human error).

The day of the flight finally arrived and I got to Moorabbin at about 0700 for a 0930 departure. I obtained the weather report and completed my flight planning and pre-flight—ready to go. Everything looked good and I departed on time with an estimated flight time of 1.5 hours. This would take me via Ballarat and Ararat then on to St.

Arnaud. The flight proceeded without a problem and I thought to myself: 'how good is this?' and that I should have got my licence years ago instead of finally doing it after reaching my so-called mid-life crisis.

On the day I planned to return to Moorabbin I first had to go into town as I did not have access to the internet. I went to an internet café, did my flight planning and submitted the plan. The weather looked CAVOK with a moderate southerly at St. Arnaud, my observation only as there is no TAF. I planned to return to Moorabbin via Bendigo, Kyneton, Kilmore and Sugarloaf reservoir. The weather for the route looked OK. There was some low cloud and reduced visibility in the late afternoon, but still above VMC, on both the area and Moorabbin forecasts. The flight home was about 1.5 hours and I planned to be back at Moorabbin at approximately 1530. After doing my pre-flight and departing on time I was feeling pretty good about how well things had gone.

On reaching Bendigo and taking up my next heading to Kyneton, in the distance to the south I could see some of the forecast low cloud. I estimated it was far enough away not to be a problem. I reached Kyneton, then turned towards Kilmore descending from 4500 ft to 3500 ft still in VMC, but cloud now looking closer, but I thought, still OK to proceed. At Kilmore I started my descent to 2500 ft due to the CTA steps and lowering cloud base. Visibility was now starting to reduce considerably, but I was confident I could still maintain VMC. Approaching Yan Yean Reservoir I estimated the visibility to be about 6000 metres and I thought to myself that this was happening much earlier than expected and seemed to be worse than the forecast. Being relatively inexperienced, I pressed on thinking I could still make it back to Moorabbin—after all it wasn't that far.

At Sugarloaf Reservoir I thought, 'I now have to make a decision whether to continue or divert,' as I could not even see the Dandenong Ranges. I decided to divert to Lilydale, gave the CTAF call and turned towards the airfield. I had never been to Lilydale aerodrome before or even seen it, but I had the information on hand, along with

Coldstream Aerodrome— pre-flight planning was paying off. In front of me I saw an airfield. 'All good,' I thought, 'I will overfly, check the windsock then land.' As I was overflying I saw the writing on the roof of the building—Coldstream! I did not know how I missed Lilydale but never mind; I decided to land. flew the circuit and landed on runway 17 without a problem. I remember thinking that I was happy to be on the ground once again as the conditions had deteriorated substantially and that perhaps I had left my decision to divert too late.

After shutting down and tying the aircraft down, I contacted the flying school at Moorabbin to tell them that I would not be back as I had put down at Coldstream. They said they had been trying to ring me to let me know that the weather had been updated and that I would be better to delay my return until the next day because I would not be able to get into Moorabbin. I left the plane at Coldstream overnight and came back to the aerodrome early the next morning, but I was still unable to get out until about 1300 and was stuck on the ground until then.

Eventually the conditions improved enough to depart and return to Moorabbin successfully. Reflecting on my flight, I was happy I had followed my instructors' advice about thorough planning, but I was disappointed with my decision to press on when I should have made the choice to divert much earlier. That saying you always hear about: 'Get there 'itis' was true. It can happen so easily, especially for the inexperienced. Lesson learnt!

NOTES:

SOMETHING TO WATCH

CASA

Name withheld by request, Mar 28, 2014

They say time flies when you're having fun...

I was off on a short flight with a friend from Cambridge (Hobart's GA hub) across to Bruny Island to have a look at some oyster farms. The day was clear, if a little cool, and glorious for flying. All went smoothly as we tracked south of the city of Hobart, my passenger enjoying the view after getting over a slight case of nerves. Seeing your own city from a light aircraft (Cessna 172 in this case) is always fun.

We landed on Bruny, enjoyed the oyster farm inspection and then took off again a couple of hours later. The plan had been to return directly to Cambridge, but we had plenty of fuel and no shortage of time, so I asked my passenger if he'd like to have a look at the D'Entrecasteaux Channel which lies between Bruny Island and the south west of mainland Tasmania. Having spent plenty of time in that area—he owned a shack a bit further down—he was very keen to see it from the air.

Why not, on such a glorious day?

I made a departure call from the Bruny strip, noting it was 'time two two'. Knowing there was plenty of fuel on board, I calculated that if we were passing this point by one zero on the return, we would be well within limits of the reserves required.

We flew south west for a bit, away from home base, tracking along the coast and enjoying the view. My passenger and I were both keen divers, so we got to chatting about the spots we were seeing, what the various mountain ranges were that we could see off to the north, and how stunning this part of the world was.

Rounding South East Cape, I checked the time again to make sure all was good. Yep, two two; plenty of time to make that one zero requirement. I decided to track a bit further up the coast, knowing that the scenery just got better and better in this remote part of the State.

Ten minutes later I figured it must be time to start heading back. I checked my watch again. Two two. That seemed oddly familiar.

'*What time is it?*' I asked my passenger. '*About ten to.*'

Bugger. For the first time in four years my watch battery had stopped.

We didn't track coastal—I simply turned the nose directly toward Cambridge and announced we'd best get ourselves back home. We still had plenty of fuel, but I'd certainly given myself a glimpse of how quickly things can go wrong.

So what should I have done? Carried a back-up watch? Nobody wears two watches. Been more aware of the time? Yes, perhaps.

What would have been far more sensible was to have planned the flight—even if just a rough, written sketch of it with some timing points written in. By just looking at my watch and expecting the one zero that would indicate a need to be at a particular point, I had no inbuilt mechanism to guard against the watch's battery life coming to an end. If I had been noting time on a written plan, it would have very quickly been obvious when I wrote the same numbers several minutes apart.

It didn't cause a problem on that short flight where the safety parameters were wide. On a longer cross-country flight, when diversion decisions could have been affected by assumed endurance, it might quickly have become serious.

The lesson is simple and one that we're all familiar with—plan the flight and fly the plan. It builds in safeguards against the most unlikely of errors.

NOTES:

IN THE DARK

CASA

Mar 18, 2015

I had originally intended to stay another day at the airshow, but an old mate camping next to me is leaving, so I decide suddenly to head home a day early. Packing up the under-wing camp takes an hour or so, and we miss the takeoff slot before an aerobatic display. While packing all the gear into my little one-seat amateur-built, I ask my mate for the time of last light. After a quick mental calculation I'm sure there's ample time for the long flight, provided the refuelling stop is pretty slippery. We've both filled up from a mobile tanker the previous day, so with gear stowed and pre-flight done, we farewell the small gathering of well-wishers, start engines and taxi towards the duty runway. The long taxi allows my engine to warm up properly and I'm impatient for the display to finish so we can take off. There's nothing like the thrill of joining a queue of aircraft lining up to head into the wild blue yonder! It takes a lot of focus to be across radio traffic, pre takeoff checks, watching for other aircraft, and keeping a taildragger in line on a windy strip. The bloke in front is off the ground and it's my turn. Check for anyone on final, fuel pump on.

Make call entering runway and departing to north. Gently ease throttle open, keep on the centre line as she gets to full power. A little back on the stick and off we go. A few seconds in ground effect to pick up speed then pull up into a 1000 ft per minute climb out. Boost pump off, steep left turn giving great view of the airshow, then off to the north. After being tossed about on climb, what a relief to get above the turbulence and cruise in silky smooth air. I have some fun flying hands free. Little plane is trimmed so well I can make subtle course corrections by moving my head. Flying north into the sun, I realise I should have cleaned the screen. Peering through a layer of bugs for a couple of hours is hard on the eyes. There's no traffic to see, except one aircraft thousands of feet below me on the same heading. He slowly pulls ahead and lands for fuel before me. We have a short yarn at the bowser. I don't get around to cleaning the screen, I don't think it should be an issue on this leg because the sun will be behind me. After a quick check of the aircraft, I'm off. The sun is low in the sky, but home is only an hour away. After climbing to cruise level, I can see the sun setting behind me and suddenly notice how dark it is up ahead. I'm still a long way from home and night is coming on faster than I expected. Whoops.

This is not good.

I fly on for a few minutes while I take in my predicament. What are my options? Turn back and camp the night at last airport? Not very safe. There's still lots of traffic around and I'd be flying into a red sunset with a dirty screen. Divert to somewhere close by? Damn! The local chart is in the luggage bay, I forgot to swap maps when I landed. My ERSA* has slipped out of reach. Keep calm and think. I remember that my phone's tracking app is transmitting breadcrumbs so my wife can see where I am. She must be worried. OzRunways** to the rescue. I look up a nearby airport I've never been to. Switch radio channels then make a dramatic 90-degree turn and head for the mountains that mark its location. Can't see the town in the gathering dusk. Bit worried. Little plane is nudging VNE as I trade height for speed – probably safe in this smooth air. Open Google Maps™ to make sure I'm on the right heading. A slight correction, then after a few nervous minutes I see the street lights. The strip should be four miles south of town. There it is, lucky to see it in this light. What a relief. Make a downwind call and a fast, sweeping approach, then the smoothest landing, and nobody to see it. Taxi up to a group of buildings, looking around with my landing lights. Shut down outside the deserted terminal, climb out – a bit shaky – and tie down, fumbling with the ropes. I phone my darling wife to tell her that I'm safely on the ground. Instead of relief and gratitude, I cop an earful. She's been watching my progress on her computer. It's after dark and she's been worried sick. Seeking a little compassion I tell her I'm starving. I missed lunch in the rush to get home to her. Here I am facing a hungry night at a lonely airfield. There's no sympathy. I've got myself into this mess, so I'm on my own. (I phone town to have a pizza delivered. Well worth the $30.) She's right. I'd stuffed up big time. What a fool I'd been. I'd made several stupid errors – a hurried departure without careful planning, and not getting an accurate time for last light. I didn't organise a viable alternate airfield. I didn't ensure I had the correct chart before takeoff. I hadn't kept ERSA within reach. The screen was dirty. I'd proven the statistics – the most dangerous time is after a pilot has become 'proficient'. Complacency had crept in and could have killed me. I could have pranged my plane in some isolated clearing – or worse. But I'd been lucky, very lucky. I could have missed all the great things in my life since that day. As often said, aviation safety lessons have been written in blood. Mine could have been added, needlessly. Learn from the mistakes of others they say – you won't live long enough to make them all yourself.

NOTES:

DOUBLE TROUBLE

CASA

by Ian Robinson and staff writers, Mar 28, 2014

It has often been said that a pilot's initial twin rating is the most risky undertaking in their flying career. This story will provide ample evidence in support of that theory.

I was only a 100-hour single-engine PPL when a cash injection allowed a visit to a small flying school, 'guaranteeing' a TR in two days for $1000. I was introduced to an Apache whose paintwork alone suggested that its performance might be just a little compromised. No matter, it was a beautiful day, and my youthful instructor was full of enthusiasm. The aircraft passed its pre-flight and off we went for an uneventful and very enjoyable first flight. After hours of C150s, the old Apache felt like a DH Mosquito! No single-engine work until the last twenty minutes, when the instructor demonstrated zero thrust, and I had my first taste of the foot forces required.

Lesson two was more of the same at altitude, but included a VMC demonstration, with a complete engine shutdown and restart using airflow. It was going well and the instructor decided on one more single-engine drill before heading back for circuit work. No problems-once again the engine was completely shut down, the prop feathered, and we began a descent.

'We'll do a single-engine approach and full stop landing as an introduction to the low-level stuff.'

It all sounded just fine at the time and our recovery to short final went by the book. However, that was where it all started to go very, very wrong.

I heard a call from the right seat of 'Short final, *$*#, no gear! Go around, go around!' I had already performed the downwind checks, and confirmed three greens gear down and locked, so I did hesitate momentarily. My man added full power on the live (right) engine and took over the controls, yelling, 'Crank it, crank it!'

We proceeded very slowly down the runway at about 30 feet, with him flying, and me watching a propeller flicking over extremely reluctantly, and the engine not starting. My memory of the next few minutes is quite likely to be partially suppressed forever, but I'm pretty certain everything was forward by this time, so there was fuel. Not as helpful though, were full flap and gear down! (Yes, it was down!)

As low-level passes go, ours must have seemed interesting to bystanders. We were not gaining height but the ground ahead of us did rise. I can remember suggesting we 'put it down' while we still had runway, but the instructor elected to turn left away from the rise. The next few memories are a series of still images and sound bites in my head. A tree, the sight and sound of the upper twigs running past the canopy, a house, a dog ... and then all was still after an incredibly soft impact on thick grass.

The next image is of the wreck, about 50 metres away!

The aircraft track through the grass suggested a large yaw angle on ground contact. We must have been very close to VMC – so any higher, and we could have rolled and impacted inverted. As I said, the gear was down, so our problem had been electrical, involving only the indicators.

Helpful people soon arrived and, after much head-shaking, I was driven to a cheap motel for the night to be ready for the Authority investigation next day. Unhurt, but pretty shaky, I decided to shower and relax. Would you believe it, the shower tap labels were reversed, so my attempts to cool the water resulted in a scalded shoulder? I had survived the crash, only to be burnt in the bathroom!

What did I learn?

A zero thrust setting is safer than a complete shutdown at low level.

Instructors can make mistakes. (Everything forward, gear up, flaps up, blue line etc. – it just didn't happen.)

An old aircraft may not perform by the book.

A controlled forced landing straight ahead would have been better than pressing on and losing control, even if the gear had been up.

Avoid cheap motels.

NOTES:

TIGER COUNTRY

CASA

by Owen Zupp and staff writers, Mar 25, 2014

On a June afternoon in 1993 I was tasked with a commercial pre-licence test for an overseas candidate who was champing at the bit to return home and join his national carrier. Clear skies, an aeroplane fresh from its 100-hourly and a diligent student set the tone for a pleasurable flight; well, for the first couple of hours anyway ...

Azlan possessed a very quiet manner that somewhat belied the fierce determination with which he approached his flying training. As he leaned over the wing of the Aerospatiale TB20 Trinidad and re-calculated his endurance and performance figures, he was a picture of concentration. We had successfully navigated our way from Bankstown to Goulburn and northwest to our present port of call, Cowra. He had flown smoothly and countered the periodic 'examiner-induced challenges' that inherently crop up during a test flight. From here it was on to Mudgee, then a return to Bankstown and hopefully a recommendation for the fully-fledged licence test. His preparation and planning had been superb and his chosen routing reflected his comprehension of my perennial pre-cursor; ' ...

bearing in mind that this is a single-engined aeroplane'. That's a philosophy highlighting the advantages of a few extra track miles over topographically friendly territory, presenting a pilot with fields and features that can assist in navigation and provide options should things go quiet up front.

With the paperwork completed and more than adequate fuel evenly distributed between the two wing tanks, we fired up and launched once more into the beautiful skies over western NSW. Once established in the cruise, I adopted the role of employer and advised Azlan that the 'passengers' at Mudgee had cancelled their flight and he was now to return to Bankstown, 'bearing in mind that this is a single-engined aeroplane'.

In the only tarnished point of the flight, Azlan guesstimated a heading and wheeled the aircraft eastward to point in the general direction of Bankstown. The proposed route was relatively featureless and characterised by the mountainous 'tiger country' of the Great Dividing Range. While seemingly a poor option, he was not breaking any rule and was acting in command under supervision (ICUS). At worst it was a questionable technique and a point for the de-briefing, which after all, is what training is all about.

I was midway convincing myself of this fact when a flickering of light caught my eye. The digital fuel flow gauge was hopping around without rhyme or reason, while the engine continued to purr and the good old-fashioned analogue fuel flow needle sat like the Rock of Gibraltar. New-fangled gadgetry, maybe, but either way it prompted me to look outside for a potential forced landing field; just in case. As luck would have it, a lone small clearing was just off the right and I asked Azlan to enter a gentle turn toward it. He had still not noticed the 'Digi-Flow' jumping around when I drew it to his attention and started to talk him through the trouble-shooting process. When the analogue needle started to reflect the readings of its digital counterpart my interest heightened and we completed an FMOST check without delay. The engine now began to surge in company with the cockpit indications, so at this point I took over and called up

Sydney Flight Service. I had gone from 'fat, dumb and happy' to 'rather concerned' in about ninety seconds.

Our lone paddock approached below, and the surges were becoming so significant that maintaining our height was becoming increasingly difficult. I advised Flight Service that we were 55DME on the Sydney 255 radial while I still could, as VHF had been 'in and out' at this height. I was contemplating a precautionary landing with the remaining sporadic power when total engine failure made the decision for me. I trimmed for the glide, and knowing VHF was at a premium, alerted Sydney of our worsening predicament and manually switched on the emergency locator transmitter (ELT). Again through the checks; no luck. Fortunately I had already decided upon the field and a course of action. I briefed Azlan and told him that when we were on the ground, he was to exit and get clear of the aircraft without delay.

Assured of making the field, I started configuring the gear and flaps and advised Flight Service that I would shortly be going 'no-comms' as I switched the electrics off in an attempt to minimise the chance of post-impact fire. The world was getting very big in the window, and as I aligned myself with the field, I decided that it was way too short to make it over the trees on the approach and still pull up by the far end. As I had done at airstrips in the outback and Papua New Guinea, I slipped the aircraft down between the trees in an effort to maximise the effective length. The foliage rushed by, there was a short squeak of the stall warning horn and then the wheels hit. Thump!

Seventy knots or so across an unprepared surface is a wild ride. I was on the brakes, keeping straight and hoping for the best when a sizeable rock jutted up ahead. Unable to swerve to any great degree, I braced, thinking 'this is going to hurt'.

I tensed my guts and for a nanosecond thought of the control column spearing into me. Bang! The right gear struck the rock and we were OK-hurtling across the paddock, but OK. With not enough room for my liking, I heaved back on the stick and kicked in right boot, effectively 'ground-looping' a nose-wheel aeroplane. The right gear seemed to give at this point and we slewed sidewards, shuddering to a halt short of the trees. I swung around to tell Azlan to get out. With the disturbed dust still suspended in the late afternoon air, I was looking at an empty seat, an open gull-wing door and the northbound end of a southbound student.

I joined my breathless candidate and having taken a moment, returned to a rather forlorn aircraft. Paranoia forced me to inspect the Trinidad's tanks, which revealed adequate fuel both sides. Phew! I tried calling up on VHF, and thankfully established contact with an approaching Cessna 310 who had already been diverted to the area. I advised the pilot that we were all OK and he relayed our exact position to Flight Service. (He had one of those new fangled GPS things.) It was getting dark, and with the temperature dropping, we threw on our jackets and gathered kindling in case we were there for the night. Fortunately, Careflight was on the job from Westmead Hospital and making a beeline through the night sky to our position. Strapped in, the rotors spun up and we rose into the absolute darkness. Slowly the glow of Sydney's lights became a visible horizon. It was at this point I think I stopped to draw a breath.

Twenty years have passed and I have applied lessons I gleaned from the experience ever since. First and foremost, my philosophy of track selection in single-engined aircraft was upgraded to a personal doctrine. Whilst recognising it is not always possible, the trade off of track miles must be made where friendly terrain is on offer. Be aware of terrain, lowest safe altitudes, airfields and NAVAIDS in the planning phase when you have the time available for consideration.

I have always had one eye out the window for a field when I've been flying single-engined aeroplanes. Those thousands of hours of looking probably only really made a difference for me on this one occasion, but it was a life full of difference. Being aware of my only option, deciding to turn towards it and formulating a potential plan before things turned totally to worms, probably saved my neck. My actions weren't the hallmark of exceptional skill; they were simply the application of the training we all receive as licence holders.

Another reason that we walked away that day was that I was current on practice forced landings, and I had a fair amount of experience on short strips with no asphalt and touch-down markers. My currency at the time was due to my job as an instructor, but ever since I have insisted on a dual check in my private flying to ensure I'm still up to speed on unexpected occurrences such as engine failures and go-arounds. Bush flying also gave me an appreciation of speed control and the feel of an aeroplane at that slower speed and of the performance envelope. It gave me a greater sense of an approaching stall than is necessarily offered by the warning devices fitted to aircraft. Again, it was an issue of currency. Even if your flying is always out of long, sealed strips, integrate some short field arrivals and departures into your comings and goings. You never know when you may need to call upon these skills.

Personally, I lost a degree of innocence in the Blue Mountains that afternoon. I had always looked upon every patch of urban clearing as a potential forced landing field, which in retrospect was a little naïve and over-confident. These days I'm a little more selective. Notwithstanding, I have continued to fly, own, and enjoy single-engined aeroplanes ever since. The experience in no way deterred me from 'singles': it merely reinforced my belief in how they should be operated.

NOTES:

CHAPTER 4

COMMUNICATE & AIR CREW

"The readiness to blame a dead pilot for an accident is nauseating, but it has been the tendency ever since I can remember. What pilot has not been in positions where he was in danger and where perfect judgment would have advised against going? But when a man is caught in such a position he is judged only by his error and seldom given credit for the times he has extricated himself from worse situations. Worst of all, blame is heaped upon him by other pilots, all of whom have been in parallel situations themselves, but without being caught in them. If one took no chances, one would not fly at all. Safety lies in the judgment of the chances one takes."

Charles Lindbergh
(Journal entry 26 August 1938)

TCAS CLIMB

CHIRP

Aug 2016, Issue 69

When on a return flight to my home airfield, I decided I would fly across the ILS approach 21 at [ ]. I usually use the overhead and talk to them, however this seemed a quicker passage and I thought if I listened in I would have a clear picture of what if anything was happening. When on frequency I heard a pilot call that he had made a TCAS climb and thought, "oh dear someone's in trouble". I felt I had been on frequency for a while and not heard any aircraft on finals.

I called the approach and passed the obligatory message including my present position and altitude. I also heard other aircraft talking to the ATC but had not seen any aircraft in spite of a constant look out.

A little later I was asked on landing to contact the tower which I duly did. To my horror it would seem that it was indeed me that an approaching [aircraft] had seen on TCAS and climbed to avoid.

I thought that 2 miles out and at 2200 ft I was comfortably above any aircraft on final, it wasn't until I was sat in my office with the [ ] approach chart that I could appreciate just how wrong I was.

I do find the Instrument Approach Chart quite difficult to interpret and feel clarity in its layout may assist other GA pilots, however had I called earlier and understood the distances and altitudes of the glideslope then I would have not put another aircraft in that position. My apologies to the [other] pilot.

My advice to any pilot would be to call an airfield you are approaching allowing plenty of time for ATC to advise you of any landing or circuit traffic. I probably would have heard the other aircraft as well had I been on frequency earlier.

In five years of flying and almost 1200 flights I have always thought I was a considerate pilot with good airmanship, just goes to show one never stops learning.

CHIRP Comment: The reporter is commended for this honest and open report. Also, by using his transponder he demonstrated good safety practice and enabled the TCAS in the other aircraft to do its job and protect them both. If his aircraft had been 2 miles out from the airfield it should have been well above the instrument glide path and clear of the aircraft on the approach. The reporter subsequently assessed that his flight log showed him around 4 miles away. However, flying anywhere in the vicinity of an airfield without contacting ATC risks conflicting with aircraft in the instrument hold, those outbound for an instrument procedure or aircraft on the approach path itself. Furthermore aircraft conducting non instrument straight–in approaches would not necessarily comply with the instrument descent profile along the feather.

Although there is a legal right to fly where you will in Class G airspace, the most sensible course of action, as recommended by the reporter, is to call on the RTF. It should be noted that the Instrument Approach Procedure (IAP) 'feathers' on VFR charts are aligned along the extended centrelines of the MAIN instrument runways and are not representative of the coverage area of the IAP associated with that runway. Furthermore, there may be IAPs to secondary runways that are not depicted by a feather. Therefore, pilots are strongly recommended to call before approaching within 10 NM of any airfield marked with one or more instrument approach feathers.

Aircraft on the approach to an airfield have no right of way in Class G airspace and must comply with the rules of the air, giving way to aircraft on their right side. Commercial aircraft are also obliged to respond to TCAS Resolution Advisory warnings (TCAS RAs) even if the flight crew believe they are in visual contact with the aircraft causing the warning. The reason is that flight crew have sometimes misidentified an aircraft they can see as the one causing the RA and had a close encounter with the one actually posing the threat. Unfortunately, in the reported incident the aircraft reacting to the TCAS RA climbed into conflict with another aircraft in the instrument hold. This reinforces the unit's preference for transiting pilots to contact them in good time and whenever possible to plan to fly through the airfield overhead.

Note 1. It is always good to try removing both headset plugs and reinserting them. Crud can build up on the contacts and this action should clean them. Once back on the ground the plugs can be cleaned properly.

NOTES:

POTENTIAL COLLISION
CHIRP

Aug 2016, Issue 69

We were en route to Sleap (EGCV) from the south east under VFR. Weather was fine with good visibility, some haze into sun. In accordance to the published arrival information contact was made with Shawbury APP to obtain MATZ clearance. Approval for MATZ penetration was received *"not below 2,100 ft"* on the MATZ pressure setting with instruction to call when Sleap in sight to request to change to Sleap A/G. At this time although there was some traffic on the Shawbury frequency it was not unacceptably busy.

At the point Sleap was sighted the Shawbury controller became engaged with another aircraft that was having some communication problems and appeared to be requesting assistance in establishing its location (the aircraft was looking for Welshpool). While this conversation was in progress as it was not possible to interrupt to request a change to the Sleap frequency and start a dead side decent to circuit height we remained at approximately 2,200-2,300 ft on the dead side of the circuit. Soon after passing Loppington contact was made with Shawbury and the frequency was changed to Sleap A/G. Sleap were advised that we were descending dead side for a standard overhead join to runway 23 left hand circuit. The A/G exchanges identified some circuit traffic but no other inbound traffic at that point.

Approximately 0.25 miles NW of the village of Burlton, while the pilot was looking for the upwind end of the active Sleap runway the front seat passenger (also a pilot) noted that the PCAS was showing an alert message and saw an aircraft on a converging heading at the same level. At the time of the incident he reported noticing that our height was 2,100 ft. The other aircraft was travelling west to east and appeared to be on a heading in the region of 080-090 at approximately the same level.

We executed a steep diving right turn to avoid contact. The other aircraft did not appear to take any avoiding action. The distance at the point of commencing the turn was thought to be in the region of 50-75 metres, although this is a retrospective subjective assessment.

Following the avoiding turn we reoriented ourselves and made a normal overhead join for runway 23.

When discussing the events on landing there would seem to have been several contributing factors: being unable to request a change of frequency from Shawbury and delayed descent from the *"not below 2,100 ft"* instruction due to the protracted exchange between the controller and the aircraft unsure of position, the higher than normal workload caused by the need to descend to circuit height while locating the runway while effecting a left turn to cross the upwind end of the active runway and finally the appearance of an aircraft that was not heard transmitting on either the Shawbury or Sleap frequencies prior to the AirProx.

Lessons Learned:

1. R/T communications should be kept to a minimum necessary for safe conduct of the flight. Should

protracted communication be necessary try to allow time for urgent/pressing messages from other aircraft to intercede?

2. ATC units need to keep track of aircraft that have been given transient instructions e.g. not below/above X until ... Having given such an instruction the control unit may reasonably expect that aircraft to reestablish communication when the condition is met and should avoid long conversations without breaks.

3. High levels of situational awareness are essential in complex ATZ configurations and the appearance of uncontrolled aircraft need to be considered.

CHIRP Comment: It seems clear that delaying the change of frequency from Shawbury to Sleap created the conditions for this AirProx. The Military Aviation Authority confirmed that the Shawbury ATCO would expect the reporting pilot to switch to the Sleap frequency at the appropriate time; the controller would be aware of the reporter's intentions, have been watching his progress on radar and would be aware that there was little opportunity for the pilot to speak on the RT to announce that he was changing frequency. Although this was a close call, the value of electronic conspicuity and collision avoidance systems (in this case PCAS) should be recognised as ultimately saving the day.

It is common in busy Class G airspace to have difficulty in finding a break in the RT to speak to ATC. Sometimes having made contact and been told to standby there is a long wait before being called back. If it becomes necessary to change frequency before a service has been established, pilots should go ahead and change. However, if a service has been established there is a risk that controllers will become concerned if they cannot contact an aircraft they expect to be on their frequency. If it becomes necessary to change frequency in these circumstances pilots can ask the next controlling agency to contact the previous one to confirm that they have moved on. Alternatively, if the frequency change was a result of reaching the planned destination it might be quicker to telephone the ATC unit after landing to explain why it was necessary to leave unannounced. Pilots should not leave a frequency unannounced while flying in CAS!

NOTES:

AIRPROX

CHIRP

May 2016, Issue 68

I was PIC of a PA28 returning from [ ] to [ ]. My passenger, also a
PPL holder, had flown outward. On the first two legs of the return
flight we were going directly into low sun and I had been flying
mainly on instruments due to the poor forward visibility, with my
passenger performing lookout. I hold an IR(R). We had been
receiving a Basic Service and a new squawk. We were flying at 105
KIAS and 2700 ft on the Brize QNH. We were tracking the 162R
outbound from DTY, which put the sun in about our 2 o'clock,
improving forward visibility significantly.

One or two minutes after the radar service changeover, at approx.
1447Z and 5 NM SE of DTY - roughly 3 NM E abeam Turweston,
my passenger emitted a sudden exclamation and several expletives. I
was confused as to what his concern was for about 5-10 seconds; then
I saw another [similar type] in my 9 o'clock flying directly away from
us and 50-100 ft (estimate) below.

My passenger was quite shaken by the incident and said that the
aircraft had appeared to be coming directly at us and was close

enough for the people on board to be visible. By the time I saw the aircraft the incident was over and it was separating from us.

The other aircraft's subsequent movement suggested it may have been on a track of about 140 degrees. We surmised therefore that it must have been approaching our starboard side from behind. The sun's position meant that our starboard visibility was still poor.

No traffic information regarding this conflict was passed to us by Brize Radar. As far as we could deduce from RT exchanges after the incident, the other aircraft was not on Brize frequency. We were unable to note its registration. We considered it might have recently departed Turweston, but given our proximity to the airfield we felt it unlikely that a PA28 could have gained sufficient altitude for the conflict.

I fully accept that responsibility for conflict avoidance is the responsibility of the PIC. However, we felt strongly that as the other aircraft would have had the sun further behind it, our aircraft should have been much more obvious to its crew than it was to us.

Lessons:

1. Lookout in the vicinity of ground-based NAVAIDS needs to be especially vigilant.
2. My passenger admitted that he may have been momentarily distracted with inputting next frequencies after the radar service handover.
3. A hand-held LPAT* is certainly worth considering. [*LPAT: Low Power ADS-B Transceiver. (ADS-B: Automatic Dependent Surveillance – Broadcast). Hand-held, battery-powered, supposedly "low-cost" receiver for airborne transponder signals. Technology apparently still undergoing trials, nothing available yet, maybe next year. See Clued Up Spring/Summer 2015.].

CHIRP Comment: AirProx incidents can be investigated more thoroughly by the UK AirProx Board (UKAB) than by CHIRP because the UKAB has ready access to radar and RT recordings and the resources to trace the pilots and controllers involved to ask for their recollection of events. Nevertheless, from the CHIRP perspective there are several aspects of the report that bear comment, including agreement with the reporter's lessons identified.

It is not clear when LPATs might become available but we encourage the fitment and use of electronic conspicuity and alerting devices The AirProx occurred in Class G airspace where the pilots in both aircraft shared an equal responsibility to see and avoid other aircraft. The reporter did not see the other aircraft in time to take avoiding action; without a statement from the other pilot, it is not clear whether he saw the reporter's aircraft and stood on his course, or whether he did not see the reporter's aircraft in time to avoid it by a greater margin, or didn't see it at all. The reporter was in receipt of a Basic Service from Brize Norton. Under this Service there was no obligation on the Brize ATCO to provide Traffic Information and he did not do so. In conditions of poor visibility and/or busy airspace it is recommended to ask for a Traffic Service; if it is not available don't expect any Traffic Information under a Basic Service.

NOTES:

ALTITUDE DEVIATION

CHIRP

Feb 2016, Issue 67

It was a rainy day with very low pressure. The altimeter setting at the field was 987 hPa (29.16). We were assigned the [ ] departure off runway [ ]. After take-off we were switched to departure where we were told climb to 5000 ft and fly heading 250. This took us off the departure and deleted the step climb from 4,000 ft to 5,000 ft.

After we levelled at 5,000 ft we were given a climb to either FL070 or FL080 (I am not 100% sure which). Close to reaching our assigned Flight Level we were queried by ATC as to whether or not we had the proper standard altimeter setting of 1013 hPa set. We then realised we had passed the Transition Altitude of 6000 ft without setting our altimeters to "STD" 1013 hPa. We promptly corrected our altimeter setting and altitude but overshot our assigned Flight Level by approximately 450 ft.

The crew is experienced with operations in Europe, and the difference between "Transition Levels" and "Transition Altitudes". Prior to the departure we briefed the "Transition Altitude" of 6,000 ft as well as set the FMS default Transition Altitude to 6,000 ft for a backup. Unfortunately we still forgot to make the correct setting at 6,000 ft and deviated from our assigned altitude.

Lessons Learned:

Things that can help us from making this same mistake in the future are:

1. Be more vigilant in basic flight deck procedures, especially when operating outside of our normal environment.
2. Listening more closely to ATC for the change in assigned altitudes from "FEET" to "Flight Levels"
3. Our checklist incorporates the altimeter setting in the "After Take-off" checklist. The addition of a "Transition" check that incorporates the altimeter setting could help prevent this error.
4. Being more familiar with the FMS. Entering a new Transition Altitude in the FMS Default page after the current flight plan is loaded will have no change on the current flight. It must be done prior to flight plan insertion.

[Alternative lesson: My suggestion to avoid this happening again is to write the transition altitude on a note card and stick it on the yoke so it doesn't get forgotten about, especially when we don't fly in Europe on a regular basis.]

CHIRP Comment: The reporting crew did not adequately monitor each other or the progress of the climb and placed too much reliance on the FMS. Fortunately the controller was on the ball and no loss of separation occurred. The report highlights a problem that can be avoided by following the advice in CAP789 Requirements and Guidance Material for Operators, Chapter 12 Flight Procedures:

5.1.3 When cleared to climb above transition altitude, a designated pilot (e.g. PF) should immediately command a change to the main altimeter subscale settings saying "Set Standard", prompting a reply from the other pilot (i.e. PM) "Standard set, passing flight level three two for flight level eight zero". (This might be repeated by the Flight Engineer/Systems Panel Operator (FE/SPO).) PF should confirm this, e.g. "Three two, cleared eight zero". (Modified procedures may have to be specified for flights that take place in airspace that has a relatively high transition altitude, e.g. in the USA.)

5.1.4 Any change made to a standby or other altimeter subscale setting should be announced by a designated pilot (e.g. PF) when it takes place, e.g. "Standby to Standard". Sometimes, this can be in response to another call or prompt, such as "Passing MFA". In other circumstances, the standby altimeter subscale setting may be set to the lowest forecast QNH for the sector in which the aircraft will be flying, in which case this change should similarly be announced.

5.1.5 Before descent, the appropriate QNH should be obtained. Preferably, the standby altimeter should have its subscale set to this QNH before the descent begins or on passing a specified flight level. This change should be announced when it takes place.

5.1.6 When cleared to descend below the transition level, a designated pilot (e.g. PF) should command a change to the main altimeter subscale settings saying "Set QNH", prompting a reply from the other pilot (i.e. PM), e.g. "One zero two four set, passing eight thousand for altitude four thousand". (This might be repeated by the FE/SPO.) PF should confirm this, e.g. "Passing eight, cleared four thousand".

NOTES:

JOINING DILEMMA

CHIRP

Nov 2015, Issue 66

Approaching North Weald (EGSX) from the north-west I was receiving a traffic service from Luton. With 10 miles to go I descended below 1500 feet to be below the Stansted CTA, secured a 'freecall' message from Luton, changed the squawk to 7010, called North Weald Radio for airfield information and gave a position report. The squawk tells Stansted ATC that the aircraft in question is in radio contact with North Weald. As expected, the active runway at North Weald was 20 with a right hand circuit. This requires the aircraft to be positioned very close to the southern edge of the Stansted SFC-3500 feet CTR airspace. So far, so good.

I was listening out for other traffic and hearing none that was a factor called to say I was joining on a right base. There was then a garbled transmission that included the word 'downwind' and the North-Weald radio operator said there was an aircraft downwind in the circuit. I could not see it; neither could my passenger in the right hand seat, who was a first-time flyer in a light aircraft. My aircraft has TCAS; there was no transponder return from the other aircraft.

Fearing a conflict I made a left turn at about rate one. I recall thinking that it would have to be a very steep turn to keep out of Stansted but intuitively decided not to do that. I was quite alarmed but did not want to transmit this to my passenger, nor did I want to be messing about with 60 degree of bank so close to the ground. I made a call to North Weald, I think that I was 'extending away from the circuit' which I imagine he, like me, understood meant I was going to clip Stansted space. After a few moments I turned back and continued onto a two mile final. The other aircraft was well ahead, already over the runway executing a touch and go. There had been no 'final' call but in response to my own 'final' call and its acknowledgement, there was a transmission addressed to North Weald radio to the effect that *the radio went very quiet for a while there*. There was a strong gusting cross wind and I can well imagine that the other pilot had been concentrating on aviating and not on communicating. However, the lack of communication, and the lack of a transponder, meant I had had no idea where he was.

I landed and taxied in, expecting to hear those dreaded words, "can you give Stansted ATC a ring on ...." But the North Weald radio operator said nothing, and neither did I, and nothing has happened since.

Thinking about it I still don't know what I could and should have done. In particular, should I have preempted a potential issue with Stansted and contacted them myself? There was absolutely no time to call them on the radio at the time, although I would perhaps have had time to punch in 7700 on the squawk had I thought of it.

CHIRP Comment: CHIRP advice to pilots joining a visual circuit is normally to join overhead. This provides an opportunity to have a good look at the airfield and assimilate the positions of all the relevant traffic. However, at North Weald there is little room for an overhead join between the jet aircraft circuit at 1000 ft QFE and the

Stansted TMA at 1179 ft QFE. Therefore an overhead join is not recommended as a matter of routine there. In the reported incident, positioning for a join on base leg and hearing an aircraft downwind, which might have been jet traffic, the reporter found himself in a tricky spot. He was correct in identifying that he had a responsibility to integrate himself into the circuit pattern already established and to give way to the aircraft on his right. However, turning left in a right hand circuit was not the best course of action since it reduced his chance of seeing the conflicting traffic downwind. His decision not to fly a steep turn was correct if he was uncomfortable performing one at low altitude. Similarly, changing his transponder squawk would have been distraction from flying the aircraft and looking out. On balance, the least bad course of action was to climb to maintain just below 1500 ft QNH (1179 ft QFE) and convert from a base leg join to an overhead join. If there was time he might also have called on the radio to determine the exact position of the aircraft downwind and whether it was a jet, thereby establishing how much airspace he had to work in while remaining below Controlled Airspace.

The best way of managing tricky situations is not to get into them in the first place. At North Weald on runway 20, with the overhead join effectively limited, there would be more options available for integrating into the established circuit pattern by planning to join downwind via the Epping VRP. It is also worth noting that, although North Weald is in the Stansted TMZ, it is home to a microlight school that operates aircraft that are not transponder-equipped. Therefore any temptation to rely on TCAS for conflict avoidance must be resisted. A good lookout is essential.

Finally, the reporter was concerned that he may have infringed the Stansted CTR. A useful landmark is the water tower next to the M11 which marks the edge of the CTR. Following any suspected infringement, a telephone call to ATC after landing is unlikely to exacerbate the situation; a timely apology can work wonders as well as eliciting immediate reassurance.

NOTES:

TWILIGHT LANDING

CHIRP

Aug 2015, Issue 65

I wish to express my gratitude to one anonymous air traffic controller who recently saved my bacon. I was on the final leg of my three-cornered cross-country solo navigation exercise. All had gone well except I was late heading back, thanks to delays at [ ]. I was returning to base and contacted Approach with a Basic Service. It was still at least half an hour from sunset but the sky quickly grew very dark as thick clouds arrived overhead from the west. Even so, at 12 miles DME I confirmed my position by reference to a motorway junction which I could recognise even through the gloom. Navigating by map and eyeball is not easy by twilight, even when car headlights show you the lie of the roads below. It didn't get easier. I was following a VOR radial, as I had done several times before. I had recently checked the Direction Indicator (DI) against the compass, which was becoming increasingly hard to read and it was also swinging about a bit; so the DI adjustment was my best guess rather than a certainty.

This is where I made the mistake of following the DI to maintain heading rather than the VOR, whose needle started to move to the left. I must have moved on to a real track some 10 or even 20 degrees off from my desired track. The VOR was telling me the truth: that I was off course by two or three miles. The DI was wrong; but with the compass impossible to see in the dusk, I couldn't correct it. And laughable though it might seem in the cold light of day, I didn't know how to turn on the instrument panel lighting that would have illuminated the compass! Neither I nor my flying instructor had ever envisaged that I would need to do so. Nor is checking the panel lighting part of the standard PA28 checklist, and I was loath to start pressing unknown buttons in the dark.

At which point the DME cut out on me (a fault I reported on landing). But out of the blue - or black, by this stage - the Approach controller called me and said I was in danger of infringing Controlled Airspace. He advised me to head south east immediately. I acknowledged the message and turned but admitted I was unsure of my position (doubly unsure because of the DME failure, though I didn't say so). So we did the QDM routine, and he gave me a heading to fly. I wasn't sure, with a misaligned DI, how much that was going to help. But not long after that - and thanks to the darkness - I could clearly see the runway lights dead ahead. I told him so, and he authorised a straight-in approach.

Lessons Learned:

Students should be shown how to turn on instrument panel and cabin lighting even when no intention of flying at night. This knowledge should be tested in the final PPL/NPPL/LAPL exams and should be included in the pre-fight check list. Pilots should be advised to carry small torch in top pocket, even when not intending to fly at night and don't be ashamed to ask for QDM at the first sign of trouble.

CHIRP Comment: A really good report in which several slices of the Swiss cheese aligned to create a difficult situation and a good save by ATC. The reporter is commended for this honest report and for correctly identifying important lessons with which we agree. We would also emphasise the importance of explaining to ATC as completely as possible the nature of any problem; help them to help you! Dealing with ATC can be intimidating for inexperienced pilots but students should be encouraged to highlight their student status and use plain English to explain a problem if the situation requires it. In the circumstances described by this reporter more explanation could have helped at the departure and destination airfields.

There are also some good lessons here for instructors and ATCOs. The reporter had been told to be airborne on this last leg of his cross country by a specified time in order to make it back to base in daylight. He was held up by ATC delays during his arrival at [ ] but checked in with his flying school Ops Manager (his own instructor was airborne with another student) with time to spare prior to starting up for the last leg. However, he was held up for 25 minutes after starting and eventually took off 9 minutes after the deadline. From a Human Factors perspective it seems likely that most pilots would do the same for the sake of 9 minutes: the domestic issues of having to retake the test, leaving the aircraft away from base, getting home by public transport would all lead most of us to press on for the sake of just a few minutes. Arguably the deadline was too tight but during the winter months it would likely have been difficult to fit everything in to accommodate the student's availability, good daylight and suitable weather. One measure that might help avoid similar situations is for instructors to telephone the ATC supervisors at land-away destinations to alert them to unusual factors regarding student flights. ATC at the departure airfield should have been aware of the status of the flight anyway from the call sign prefix and might have questioned the departure so late in the afternoon; however, a phone call could have raised the profile and, in this case, perhaps ensured departure before the deadline. Furthermore it is good practice for any pilot planning a land-away to telephone his destination shortly before departure to introduce the movement and check on late warnings etc. For another example see the report later about Communication and Cockpit Organisation.

NOTES:

COCKPIT COMMUNICATION
CHIRP

Aug 2015, Issue 65

Preparing for the flying season, I created new Word documents to better organise my flights. My first time using these new documents was a flight to [ ]. Weather was CAVOK and 40k+ visibility. On approaching my destination, service was terminated by [Area] Information and I contacted [ ] using my shiny new sheet of frequencies, created just a couple of days before on xxx.475. This frequency was incorrect and I should have been xxx.45. A typo.

However, I have flown into [ ] many times before and the A/G service is not always manned. So, I continued with blind calls on the wrong frequency, keeping a good look out as I have done before.

Surprise. I was met by the airport manager who challenged me about my actions (he did, however, accept my explanation). There was parachuting at the aerodrome that day, so he was obviously concerned for safety.

Lessons Learned:

Be careful when creating self-briefing documents. I see myself as meticulous, but made a mistake in transposing a frequency from Map/Pooleys to the Word document.

Double check frequencies against the Map/Pooleys if no 2 way comms made. I trusted myself in this case as I was quite used to [ ] not being manned. Unfortunately, it was one of those times where contact was almost a necessity due to the parachuting.

No real safety issues as I maintained normal good look out on approach and in the circuit, and it was at my discretion (A/G 'Radio' frequency). However, I think a couple of lessons on organisation and communication well learned today.

CHIRP Comment: How frustrating that well intentioned and conscientious preparation for the new season should turn out badly! The majority of accidents in aviation are the result of human errors and transcription errors are very common; it is always better to cut and paste if possible. Alternatively NATS publishes cockpit-size frequency charts as part of the 28-day AERAC updates. It is good practice to telephone any land-away destination – just in case. In this occurrence the reporter would most likely have been told about the parachuting and would then have been more suspicious when there was no reply on the RT. Whenever there is no reply on the RT the assumption should be that there has been a mistake dialling the frequency or there is a problem with the radio. That there is nobody there is the last option because it has potentially the most serious consequences if incorrect.

NOTES:

ALERT TO THE DANGER
CASA

May 13, 2015

Funny how a chance discussion with another pilot before and after a flight can bring home some important safety lessons. This lesson was about avoiding the hazards associated with flying in the vicinity of non-controlled aerodromes ('alerted see-and-avoid').

I fly out of Tyabb Airport on the beautiful Mornington Peninsula south of Melbourne. Recently, when walking to my Cessna 172 to do the pre-flight checks, another pilot stopped me and asked if I could help with the lock on his aircraft door. During our quick discussion he mentioned that he had been ill, and that today was to be his first flight, taking a friend, in quite a while.

I wished him well and continued to my aircraft, casually thinking, 'I hope he flies the plane better than he gets into it', and 'hope he's OK after not flying for a while'. (I also thought about 'must be cleared by a DAME if impairment was for 30 or more days' and 'must not fly as PIC with passengers unless at least three take-offs and landings in previous 90 days').

After take-off I noted that we appeared to be the only two aircraft flying at that time. As he had taken off and departed the circuit before I finished my pre-start checks, my radio was not yet on, so I missed his radio calls. I thought that perhaps I should have asked him where he was going to fly that day (situational awareness).

On returning from solo practice in the training area over French Island, Westernport Bay, I made an inbound radio call including my position and altitude. A few seconds later there was an inbound radio call from another pilot giving the same position and altitude as me. I recognised his call sign: it was the pilot I had briefly spoken to before take-off. But there was no mention from the other pilot that he had my aircraft in sight ('If you haven't sighted the traffic, say so').

I quickly did some extra scanning in all directions, but could not see him. I thought that we could be very close to each other, and maybe closing. I instinctively turned on all my remaining outside lights, and after an extra-good scan, turned away from the airport in a gentle left-hand 360 degree turn to get well out of the way ('Turn on external lights in vicinity of non-towered aerodromes' and 'change heading to create relative movement to help detection and avoid collision').

I still could not see him, but then I heard his radio call joining the circuit mid-downwind, so I knew he was now well in front of me and well out of the way. On overflying the airport before descending to circuit height on the dead side and joining crosswind, I heard his base and final radio calls and could easily see him.

Back on the ground we had another brief discussion. He said he first saw me with all my outside lights on turning to the left. He had been well behind me, a little higher and slowly descending ('look before descending!').

I thought later that perhaps after his inbound radio call I could have made a radio call asking him if he had me in sight, but recognising that we could be very close and closing, I judged that time was of the essence and so I opted to do what I did ('aviate, navigate, communicate'). It worked and I reckon I did the right thing. I know my inbound call was accurate in terms of position and altitude, but I am not so sure about his.

NOTES:

A FEW HOME TRUTHS
CASA

Mar 28, 2014

I was 40 years old before I could achieve a long-time ambition to fly. Over the next 20 years as a PPL holder I managed a few hundred hours on Cessna's and Pipers, gaining a night VMC rating and a formation flying endorsement. Now nearing 80 years old, and no longer flying, I can only look back on my excellent formal training and on the informal advice from more experienced pilots that enabled me to do this without even scratching an aircraft or scaring a passenger.

You can learn a lot about safety by listening to hangar talk. What do you do on a 'touch and go' when the full flaps refuse to retract and the end of the short strip is fast approaching? Recycle the flap settings – that sometimes works. It did for me. What happens on a cold starry night at 5,000 feet, miles from anywhere, when the previously smoothly purring single engine begins to cough and splutter? Apply full carby heat and hope any ice is melted quickly. Again, that worked for me. Acting as check pilot during club competitions in a venerable Cessna 150, what is the correct protocol when the ex-RAAF PIC with thousands of hours on the most sophisticated aircraft, but few on the Cessna, is about to 'go round' with full flap extended? Say 'flaps' very firmly and audibly. And we cleared the trees bordering the country strip with room to spare.

Sometimes, however, a problem arises which you have not heard discussed. One occurred when as a student I was completing my final five-hour navigation exercise to gain an unrestricted licence.

The instructor arrived at the field late, but I had prepared well in advance and we took off soon after.

Three incidents occurred during the flight, none of which I really understood until several days later.

I had planned for BO50 but my instructor told me to climb to 9500 ft, saying he would do the necessary communication with ATC. I was happy to 'aviate' and' navigate', leaving the 'communicate' part to him. Soon after reaching the new level I heard a mildly reprimanding ATC on the radio telling us that we were on the incorrect frequency, and should change to the one he was giving us. Embarrassing, but not really my problem. I thought the instructor was using the incident to impress upon me the importance of correct communication. He definitely succeeded.

Arriving over a country airport where a landing was planned I was meticulous in letting down to circuit height on the 'dead' side, and accurately flying the crosswind and downwind legs. I was really anxious to impress this instructor. Imagine my horror when on turning base to finals I was asked, 'do you intend to land downwind?' The windsock clearly showed I was landing into wind. I pointed out this fact to the instructor who then agreed with me and we landed uneventfully. Once again I assumed this was part of the test I was undergoing to become an unrestricted pilot.

Fuel checks on the ground showed we had sufficient fuel for the flight home. Back in the air I was given an unexpected diversion to an unknown locality. I thought I handled the diversion well. Just 15 minutes out from home base I was feeling comfortable with my day's performance. True, the instructor had not said much on the flight but we were not there to chat; my job was to convince him that I flew well enough for my licence restriction to be lifted. Suddenly with no warning the engine stopped. From the startled look on the instructor's face I knew this was no test.

It was the only time before or since that I have had an engine quit on me in flight. The silence is awesome. In less time than it takes to tell, I recognised the cause of the engine failure and fixed the problem by reaching down and changing fuel selection from left to right tank on the console of the Cessna 172. The engine immediately started. I had run the left tank dry.

Before that day I had always flown with fuel selection on both, ignoring the left/right switches. On this flight the instructor overrode my choice, saying that tanks should be alternated each 30 minutes for a more balanced flight. He took it upon himself to make the change, doing so several times – and with no real choice I was not going to argue with him. But somehow in the final stages of this flight he forgot to make the switch. The left tank was exhausted. No harm was done, as the other tank held adequate fuel. I completed the day's exercise successfully.

A few days later I found out why my instructor, normally really sharp with his instruction, had been so far off his game as to make three errors with a student, one of which (at least) could have been serious and all of which were embarrassing and unnecessary.

That morning, before he set off for the training aerodrome, he and wife had argued seriously enough for the D-word to be used. He had spent the day in a highly emotional state of mind. Sitting beside me for five hours with little to do but chew over his worries he became even more preoccupied with his domestic problems and less aware of what he was doing.

The safety lesson I learned that day has not been forgotten. Flying demands total concentration. Emotional worries and personal concerns must not be taken into the air. And, most definitely, there must be no fight with the wife before flight.

NOTES:

CHAPTER 5

WEATHER & WIND

"There is no reason to fly through a thunderstorm in peacetime."

Sign Above Squadron Operations Desk

Davis-Monthan AFB, AZ

1970

EDGING AROUND THE STORM
CASA

Name withheld by request, Jan 11, 2017

As someone who grew up in south-eastern Queensland, I will always remember the strong summer storms that would blow through: the intensity and sheer power of these storms always had me sitting on the verandah mesmerised by the sight of horizontal rain, wind gusts that would double over the big gum trees and lightning that sounded like it was mere metres away.

Many years later, after several seasons of flying commercially, I was well aware of just how destructive these storms could be. Aviation is littered with tragic tales of the destructive power of these impressive feats of nature, and as a pilot I always felt it was important to take heed of these stories and not end up as a statistic.

This day in November I was about to see the true power of a summer storm that would etch itself into Brisbane's recent history.

The flight was straightforward enough; departing Brisbane I would be tracking to the Gold Coast, to pick up guests for an aerial real estate inspection before dropping them off and returning to

Brisbane, Archerfield. Forecast weather was typical for this time of year, hot clear conditions with TEMPO TS to affect the area and aerodrome in the afternoon. Fuel planning was no issue as I had plenty of capacity for trip fuel, holding and an alternate to the north if I got boxed in.

The first half of the flight went as planned. The ride was slightly bumpy from thermal activity, but apart from a slightly delayed departure from the Gold Coast as a result of late arriving passengers, nothing was abnormal. On return to the Gold Coast to drop the passengers off I could see the weather building, a large CB (cumulonimbus) was visible on the other side of the range. This one looked different though—instead of tracking east as most of the storms do, this one was tracking north. I did a quick check of the forecast and apart from TEMPO being added to the TTF (trend type forecast) at Brisbane there was no change. I looked at the radar and could see it was a fairly intense storm. Doing a quick calculation, I worked out a rough ground speed it was travelling at and concluded I could make it back to Brisbane before the storm hit.

Fuelled up, I departed the Gold Coast, and immediately on getting airborne and climbing through 1000 ft I could see just how intense and large this storm was. It literally filled my entire field of view to the west and had tops well over 30,000 ft. While tracking northbound from the coast, I could see I was going to be able to get in front of the storm before I would eventually have to track west for Archerfield. With such a violent storm off to my left, I was actually surprised with how smooth the conditions were; I feel this lulled me into a slight sense of comfort, though.

Once I turned west I could now see just how large the storm front was. It was as black as night and filled the valley from the Gold Coast to Boonah. While there was lightning and I knew that I didn't want to be within 10 NM of the front, I still felt at this stage that I could make an attempt to Archerfield: it was clear weather to the north and I knew that if conditions worsened I could head to

Brisbane or Redcliffe. Tellingly perhaps, there was no one else in the pattern at Archerfield as I arrived into the zone. Everyone on the ground knew just how intense this storm was going to be and they were busy getting aircraft into hangars. Approaching from the southeast I joined a base for runway 04R—and the turbulence finally started to hit. The storm front was now less then 10 NM from me and I was seeing large fluctuations in wind direction, and rain that was reducing visibility by every minute.

On turning final I estimated I was within 5 NM of the rain curtain and I had to use full range of throttle movement to establish a constant airspeed as I struggled to maintain wings level. I managed to touch down and quickly raised the flaps and slowed as rapidly as possible to reduce the risk of having a wing raised by wind gusts. The storm was literally at the edge of the airfield as I shut the engines down. I got the aircraft under cover as the rain hit.

This storm would go on to destroy tens of millions of dollars of property as one of the worst hailstorms to hit the Brisbane area in decades. Many aircraft at Archerfield were torn from their ground anchors and destroyed.

It took a few weeks for me to properly reflect on what had occurred. In retrospect, I should never have turned west while tracking north from the Gold Coast. I had had a great view of the storm and its intensity and also had the luxury of multiple aerodrome choices to the north. Although I had been successful in getting the aircraft home safe and sound, it could easily have been a very different story. One strong gust of tailwind on final could have spelt disaster.

I had always felt I had a very strong respect for storms, but it wasn't until I flew so close to one that I realised why severe weather should always be given a wide berth. No matter what your skill level or your hours, you have to set yourself limitations and parameters that you and your aircraft can manage safely. And if the weather impinges on this in any way, then go to your alternate, or delay your departure.

Watching a storm's beauty from the ground will always be better then being in the air and wishing you were somewhere else.

NOTES:

CARBS AND CALORIES

CALLBACK

Nov 2016, Issue 442

[We] departed on an IFR flight plan to our home base with four souls on board.... The takeoff was normal, in rain, [with] low visibility and ceiling. [I was]...cleared to 7,000 feet. All [was] normal until approaching 5,000 feet when [the] engine was not developing climb power. [I] turned on the carb heat with no noticeable change, then turned it off after four to five minutes. [I] turned on [the] electric fuel pump, changed tanks, and adjusted the mixture, [all] with no change. I did not check the magnetos. [I] was able to hold altitude at this time but [with] little or no climb. I told ATC that we had a problem and wanted to return. He replied that the weather had deteriorated at [our departure, but another airport] had better conditions and was closer. I accepted that recommendation, and he began vectoring us [for the] ILS.... I turned on the carb heat again, but engine power continued to worsen. I couldn't hold altitude or airspeed, [and the] controller advised [us that] he didn't show any roads or fields near our position. I broke out at about 400 feet AGL and landed in a farmer's plowed and very muddy field. [There were] no injuries, and no damage occurred to the plane. No cause has been determined at this time, but I think carburettor ice could be a likely reason. Perhaps I missed signs and should've turned it on earlier or left it on longer, or perhaps the carb heat didn't work as designed.

NOTES:

CAUGHT ABOVE CLOUD

CHIRP

Aug 2015, Issue 65

I went to the airfield yesterday with a friend of mine. The idea was to fly to the coast, land out at a local field for a cuppa, then return to base.

The weather wasn't brilliant and a low cloud base delayed our departure, but it started breaking up as forecast and the blue bits of sky started opening up all around us. So, we got in the [flex-wing], and set off for a quick circuit. The cloud base was about 1000 ft and we quickly went through a hole and climbed above, and were above at about 2000 ft, looking out over this very clear layer of cloud, but all time in sight of the surface. We dropped down under the cloud, then scooted back to base to fill the tank and make sure we were all set for the trip.

Off we set, climbed above again, it was much nicer up there, and I navigated to the coast via Sky Demon and the roads on the ground. However, as we approached the coast the cloud thickened and we started to lose sight of the ground, so we turned round and went back home. When we got there, it was completely closed in. We could not see the ground at all. In a panic, I went for a gap in the clouds that looked like a deep valley does from the air. My thoughts being that it wouldn't be far through that valley to the underside of the clouds. We were then totally blacked out in cloud and at that point I thought "stuff this" and decided to climb. I jammed my foot on the throttle and pulled the bar straight and watched the compass to try and keep flying straight. This I couldn't manage because the compass was the other orientation, and turning left had the wheel going the other way. I didn't have a clue what sort of speed we were doing, or which way was up, but we must have been close to VNE, the wind noise indicated it.

Now we weren't going up with my foot jammed on the throttle, we were going down, and reflecting on it now, we must have done a sort of wing over as I tried to climb, but anyway, suffice to say we popped out of the bottom of the clouds within about 10 or 20 seconds. As soon as I saw the ground I steadied the ship and scooted back to the airfield with my legs literally shaking.

It could have easily been fatal. The airframe was under a lot of stress, I've just checked the log on Sky Demon and the maximum speed reached on the flight was 124 mph. That must have been in the spiral dive.

Note to self: stay close to the airfield in those conditions, and if the holes start closing up, find one and get below ASAP. That's what I would have/should have done differently and all would have been fine.

Lessons Learned:

If climbing above cloud, always keep an eye on the clouds and if it starts to close up, get down ASAP and land out if necessary. Better to be alive hitch hiking than dead flying.

CHIRP Comment: A close shave! Thank you for this honest and open report which contains some excellent reminders about the dangers associated with climbing through holes in the cloud. We agree with the reporter's summary of what he should have done differently and add a few additional points for anyone who, despite their best efforts, is caught out in a similar way. The overriding point is that anyone who is not qualified to fly in cloud should avoid risking having to do it. This would begin with a good aviation met forecast. For those who have not seen it, the Met Office offers a free General Aviation service which provides textual and graphical information. When considering the weather, the legal limits for VFR must be adhered to but it is important to consider what is sensible and fun; flying in very poor weather is unlikely to be enjoyable.

Once you are airborne, NEVER climb above cloud with a base so low that you can't pick a landing field when you get back down through the gaps, and carry enough fuel to allow for having to divert around the cloudy areas. If above cloud always look around, including behind you, to make sure the gaps are still big enough; do not rely on "it was OK when I left". 'With the surface in sight' should mean you always have a landable field visible, not just a bit of ground. How much cloud cover you accept is down to your own personal risk appetite. A reasonable compromise is that scattered cloud may be acceptable but broken would not, so if you can't see more ground than cloud, don't push it.

If you do get caught out, don't panic. Stay in visual flight conditions and consider your options. It may be best to climb higher if you can to allow you to see gaps at a longer range (you do have lots of fuel, don't you?) If you have a radio call D&D to check for an area of gaps, or of suitably high cloud base. There can be a natural reluctance and embarrassment to admit on the RT that you need help but this is a crucial decision point. It is far better to seek help early than to wait until you are out of options. Remember, D&D and all the resources they can bring to bear are there to provide you with assistance as soon as you ask for it.

If you decide you have to descend through cloud, set the aircraft up straight and level in trim. Reduce power steadily and sort out yaw prevention and control positions while still in clear air, and try to stay relaxed as you descend. Do not watch the cloud segments passing you. Flex-wings are very stable and provided the cloud is not too turbulent the aircraft will descend nicely in a straight line without any intervention from the pilot. Try it for yourself and practise in clear air to gain confidence. Hopefully you will never need to do it for real!

NOTES:

RUNNING FROM THE STORM
CASA

Name withheld by request, Jul 8, 2015

Pressing on into an approaching storm-front, then going into low level 'turn and run' mode; this was as close to a terminal accident in a light aircraft as I ever want to get.

As a general aviation LAME I have experienced, and generally enjoyed, many away-from-base rescue missions in light aircraft, piloted by a variety of people ranging from flying instructors to private pilots. Some of them I knew well, others not at all. I have learnt to 'expect the unexpected' and adopt certain self-preservation measures, such as being aware of where we are in respect to where we are intending to end up, and always confirming that the 'gear' is where it should be before landing (I find myself listening carefully for that, even travelling by large jet). This also includes noticing whether fuel management is happening (or not).

This flight was a short-notice trip from Jandakot Airport in Perth, WA to a remote mine site in the southeast corner of the state's Pilbara region, taking a main-wheel assembly to replace one on a Navajo which had deflated overnight.

The 'rescue' aircraft was an early M20J Mooney, the 'driver' a CPL I didn't know. The non-stop flight to the mine site was uneventful, in clear VFR conditions. Arriving just a few minutes behind plan I was advised I had less than 20 minutes to jack the Navajo, change the main-wheel and be loaded in the Mooney ready for departure. Otherwise we would miss legal last light.

We missed the deadline, by about two minutes. The pilot's call was not to risk pushing the limit in case we hit a kangaroo and the insurance company refused the claim, and the other obvious risks to his licence etc. Hard to argue with that!

We overnighted at the mine site, knowing that a cold front was forecast to cross the coast (and our return path) around 2 am local time, likely creating low cloud, rain and gusty winds for hundreds of kilometres north and south of Perth. We made an additional fuel stop at Meekatharra the next morning in case of diversion, and headed west. Not surprisingly we encountered increasingly adverse weather overhead, and began descending to remain VFR below it.

As we continued to descend, and becoming increasingly concerned, I asked the pilot was he IFR rated. 'Yes,' he stated. Has the aircraft been IFR rated in the past? 'Yes—it was maintained to IFR standards until a few months ago,' he added.

'Why don't you advise Flight Service of our situation, tell them you need to go IFR rather than keep descending, and ask to be radar-vectored into Perth?' I suggested.

Not being a pilot, no doubt there is a lot I didn't know. The pilot twice refused my suggestion without explanation and made a 180-degree turn to the east to try and out run the front while further descending—both of us looking anxiously for the Ballidu airstrip. I estimate that we were down to less than 500 feet AGL when I saw the airstrip disappearing behind our starboard wing-tip. With a hurried steep turn we did a successful straight-in approach and landing, and watched the weather close in all around us as we taxied off the runway.

The rest was anti-climactic. We waited until the weather

permitted us to continue the flight safely and legally to Jandakot Airport where we unloaded and went our separate ways.

No apology, or even explanation, was offered.

I didn't pursue the matter, but even 10 years or so later this incident remains the only time I can remember when I felt genuinely concerned that I may be about to end my life in an aircraft accident.

What lessons arose from this incident?

For me, don't assume the obvious; since we both knew about the approaching frontal weather system I had good reason to ask what 'Plan B' my pilot had if the weather was impenetrable VFR.

Crew resource management was in play when we were looking for the emergency-landing airfield, but apart from that I felt like a spectator, remote from the pilot although seated side-by-side in a four-seat single-engine aircraft, while having the strong feeling that both our lives were in imminent peril.

I guess most victims of aircraft accidents don't get to sit next to the pilot, and may be quite unaware of the impending danger until it unfolds in disaster. More discussion with the pilot during the outbound, uneventful, flight may have allowed each of us to get a feel for the nature, experience and background of the other person, which may have opened the lines of communication when the later flight became a situation of considerable tension and anxiety.

So in future 'short-notice rescue flights' I intend to be more assertive about conducting some kind of interview early in the preparations or the flight, so we both have a better idea of who the 'crew' are, in case we need to activate some 'CRM'!

NOTES:

CAVOK CONFUSION
CASA

Mar 25, 2014

CAVOK... thank goodness for that. It had been a long time since I'd seen that on a forecast. (For the uninitiated, it means ceiling and visibility are OK.) I had been hanging out on Groote Island for three wet and miserable days. This wasn't part of the plan, and what a meticulous plan it had been. We had left Bankstown seven days before on the trip of a lifetime: my mother, my best buddy's parents and I. My IFR instructor was supposed to come with us, but she had to pull out at the last minute with the comforting words... 'It's the dry season, you'll be lucky to see a cloud!'

I had pulled off a trifecta. I had planned an awesome trip around Australia in a Partenavia; my passengers were going to help pay for my trip, and a multitude of multi-command hours; and, at the last minute, I had been approached by the owner of an immaculately refurbished Cessna 310 who wanted some hours on it and had given me the most awesome rental rate. Until then I had only flown for 250 hours. I had to pinch myself at my luck.

I planned the trip thoroughly: every overnight, every tour, every fuel stop, every alternate. Nothing was left to chance.

I completed my C310 endorsement in good time, and was impressed that it was fitted with a Trimble 2000 GPS. I read the manual, but my instructor assured me that if I could use the direct-to (DTO) function, I would have it made.

At last, we departed Bankstown and settled back into the huge, newly leather-upholstered seats of the immaculate 310. Lunch at Bourke, overnight at a farm-stay near Cunnamulla. Day two, lunch at Burke and Wills Roadhouse, refuel at Burketown, dodge a few clouds and up to Sweers Island for some fresh barra fishing.

Then the heavens opened.

We had planned three days on Sweers Island, but after 24 hours, the dirt strip was so waterlogged that I decided we had better leave while we could, make a fuel stop at Borroloola, then head up to Jabiru for the night.

It was pretty clear over water, but every attempt to cross the coast to Borroloola was met with a wall of cloud almost down to the ground. After several attempts I elected to divert to Groote Island. A sealed strip and fuel were what I needed right then.

Fuelled and watered, weather checked and several local pilots consulted; it was apparent that we would not be flying VFR to Jabiru any time soon. We found a hotel. Next morning was no better. By lunchtime, my tourists were getting a little frustrated, so I put them on an RPT flight to Darwin. At least I wouldn't have the peer pressure to contend with, but I was starting to feel like a goose.

Next day it was decided that I would fly directly to Kununurra, so my passengers could get an RPT flight to meet me there, after taking a few tours out of Darwin.

Day three on the island and bingo ... Kununurra was finally CAVOK!

I set off into blue skies. The cloud had abated, but not disappeared, and was far more stratiform. A scattered layer at about 2000 feet thickened up and raised a little as I hit DTO Tindal, with clearance given at 8000 feet. I was making good time, and with no pax, I had heaps of fuel for my trip. I noticed that I was now over a solid layer of cloud. I was VFR on top, what could go wrong? I was on the radar, tracking direct to Tindal by GPS. I passed over Tindal and hit DTO Kununurra, thinking nothing of it when Tindal asked me if I was IFR capable. Tindal passed me over to Brisbane and when they asked me what my endurance was I felt a bit worried.

All of a sudden it dawned on me-CAVOK; who doesn't expect clear blue skies, light winds and perfect flying conditions? Thinking about it though, didn't it actually mean no cloud below 5000 feet, or the highest 25 NM? Well, I was at 8000 feet, and there was a layer of cloud between both those altitudes and me. I also did not have an instrument rating.

The rest of that flight was a nightmare. As I sweated, it looked as though the cloud was thinning, but was this just a mirage? While I contemplated my options, and indeed my possible fate, the cloud thinned out and by the time I got to Kununurra, it was completely SKC (sky clear).

Three days in Kununurra and the dry season set in. We didn't see a cloud for the rest of our trip. It was awesome.

I learnt many things on that trip, and am now an airline pilot of 5000 hours, but I have never learnt a lesson as well as the difference between CAVOK and SKC. If just one person who reads this loses the fanciful vision of blue skies down to the ground when they see CAVOK on a forecast, it will have been worth me telling this tale.

NOTES:

BAD WEATHER CIRCUITS

CHIRP

Nov 2013, Issue 58

A FISO reports that an aircraft reported inbound from the South was given R25LH QFE. The pilot requested a downwind join for R25LH. The pilot subsequently reported on final but could not be observed from the tower as the WX to the east was estimated cloud base 400 ft and visibility estimated as poor. WX to the west of the airfield was better, estimated OVC020 5000m. The aircraft was subsequently observed landing on RO7. Fortunately due to the poor weather there were no other flights airborne in the ATZ. (All of the RTF is recorded and confirms the information given and read back by the pilot).

Thirty minutes later Farnborough Radar passed details of an inbound aircraft that was diverting from its original route due to the weather. Farnborough Radar had previously passed the airfield details of R25LH + QFE, and these were re-iterated to the pilot on first contact with the FISO.

The aircraft was observed over the western airfield boundary and the pilot stated that he was joining downwind. The flight proceeded to the R25LH dead side and the pilot was informed that he was wrongly positioning and that the circuit details were R25LH. There was no read-back from the pilot who proceeded to fly a right hand circuit for R25, which is over the noise sensitive area and landed on R25.

A weather front was passing through decreasing the visibility and cloud base and appears to have affected both of these flights.

CHIRP Comment: This report involved two pilots electing to make non-standard approaches due to adverse weather/low cloud at an airfield with a FIS. The FISO had no responsibility for the aircraft whilst airborne except to provide information; a FISO cannot 'clear' a pilot to join downwind. In the situation described, the responsibility for the safe operation of the aircraft was solely that of the pilots involved. It was not unreasonable for the pilot who had diverted to this airfield to elect to fly a non-standard RH circuit in order to avoid adverse weather. However, both pilots should have transmitted their intentions for the benefit of other pilots in the vicinity. If the situation demands it, pilots also have the option of declaring an emergency to alert other pilots and ATC to their situation.

NOTES:

CHAPTER 6
CONTROLLED AIRSPACE

"You're gonna have to key the mike, I can't see you when you nod your head."
Transmission from Chicago's O'Hare field
Reprinted with the permission of John Carr
NATCA
www.skygod.com

POSSIBLE INFRINGEMENT

CHIRP

May 2017, Issue 72

I called [ ] ATC asking for a Basic Service. I was given the QNH which I entered into my altimeter; Sky Demon and GPS confirmed the same altitude - 2400 ft. After approximately 4 minutes I was called by [ ] ATC warning me that I was about to enter their controlled airspace at 2600 ft (controlled airspace minimum 2500 ft). I informed them that my instruments confirmed that my altitude was 2400 ft. ATC asked to change to Mode A! Due to my relative low hours I had no idea how to change from Mode C to Mode A. I therefore switched off my transponder and immediately descended to 2000 ft.

On reaching [destination] I spoke to the avionics engineer about my recent experience. *"Ha,"* he said, *"your encoder is transmitting the wrong reading!"* Now I know more detail about my transponder, which at the time was reading 200 ft out. On my next local flight I called [ ] ATC for an altitude check which now confirmed a 100 ft error (Understand the maximum acceptable error is 200 ft).

I wonder how many other GA pilots have Infringed/Not Infringed due to their transponder error.

Lessons Learned:

1. Having completed my flight training and gaining my PPL in [ ] hours I had no idea how to change to Mode A (Lesson Learnt).
2. Never fly close to Controlled Airspace.
3. Periodically ask ATC to confirm your transponder altitude reading.
4. Would I have really infringed or not?

CHIRP Comment: The aircraft equipment is one element in the transponder system and there is always the possibility of an error or fault. Therefore it is advisable, when at liberty to choose one's altitude and/or route, to allow a comfortable margin from Controlled Airspace. Doing so has the added benefit of requiring less concentration on height keeping and more capacity for navigation and lookout. Pilots should routinely fly with Mode C/Altitude selected on but occasionally, if the aircraft's Mode C is out of tolerance, ATCOs may ask for it to be switched off/Mode A selected. Therefore pilots must know how to use the various modes of any equipment they plan to use. The accuracy of aircraft transponders is checked annually as part of the airworthiness requirement for certification and permits to fly. There is no harm in asking for verification from ATC periodically - provided it isn't carried out to excess.

NOTES:

ATC MIS-CONTROL

CHIRP

May 2017, Issue 72

On his NPPL navigation test, my candidate chose a direct route, just inside the edge of [ ] MATZ and asked for a MATZ crossing. He was tentative in his RT, but made a correct initial call, after which he was told to 'standby'. Eventually he was told to pass his message, which was not very accurate but included the request to transit the Zone en route to [turning point]. The aircraft has no SSR. The controller told us to set [ ] QFE, and asked us to turn East for identification. I asked to continue on course to allow the navigation test to continue, and gave our position as 2 miles north of [a disused aerodrome marked on the ICAO 1:500,000 chart]. The controller said he needed to observe our turn before he could give Zone transit, and he could not accept my reported position since he did not know where [the disused airfield] was. He stated categorically that he would vector us back to our track once the identification was complete.

The candidate chose to follow the controller's instructions. 2 or 3 minutes later the controller advised us that we could 'resume own navigation'. No assistance was offered at this time. Shortly afterwards a different controller took over the position who also did not provide vectors back to our track. I am concerned that the treatment my candidate received in this case is likely to discourage him in future from contacting an Air Traffic Control unit with the attendant safety benefits which such contact provides. As a civilian aircraft we did not need clearance to cross the MATZ (in fact we never entered it because of the 'identification turn'), so I hold that the identification was unnecessary. Certainly the LARS controller should be able to identify ground features marked on the CAA chart of his local area. The hand-over was apparently inadequate, because the promise of vectors to return to track was not kept.

Lessons Learned:

The lesson my candidate learned was to avoid talking to [ ] ATC at all costs!

RAF Safety Centre Comment: The event appeared to be as a result of high-workload for the LARS controller coupled with a potential misunderstanding from the [reporting aircraft] crew (they were informed that they could resume own navigation with a MATZ crossing, however, they maintained their heading - possibly expecting a vector to regain their initial track). To alleviate ATC workload, a handover between LARS controllers occurred, resulting in a second controller contacting the [reporting] crew some 4:30 mins after the call to resume own navigation. It is obvious from the tone of the CHIRP report that the originator is disappointed with the service provided by the LARS controller. However, this opinion may stem from a number of misapprehensions including:

- The ability for ATC controllers to determine an aircraft's location (ATC displays do not display ½ mil charts for controlling aircraft and [the disused airfield] is not a recognised VRP).

- The requirement for the identification turn (the aircraft was not transponder equipped and required identification to ensure they were deconflicted with traffic in the [ ] visual circuit).

- Permitted actions following a clearance to "resume own navigation" (although there may have been an expectation that a specific heading would have been provided to regain track, this was not requested by the pilot).

The Regional Airspace User Working Group provides a valuable opportunity to air safety concerns and develop a greater understanding of the requirements of users and service providers. For further information of the nearest Airspace User Working Group see below.

Although the report originator may be disappointed with the service provided in this instance, it is reassuring that the aircraft was in communication with LARS and had requested a MATZ crossing. Communication between military ATC units and civilian traffic is encouraged, wherever practicable, to ensure safety for all air users operating within or in close proximity to a MATZ. I hope that this précis [of the investigation report] serves to reassure you that the RAF takes such incidents seriously and strives to reduce Flight Safety risks wherever we are able.

CHIRP Comment: The response from the RAF Safety Centre reflects the importance the RAF attaches to investigating comments about the service provided by its controllers. Military controllers typically change locations far more frequently than their civilian counterparts and may not be as familiar with the surrounding area as a civilian controller. It is important therefore, for pilots (and controllers!) to refer only to large geographic features or published references. It is also worth reminding ourselves that controllers, just like pilots, may be inexperienced in their role as well as location. It is necessary for controllers to positively identify aircraft without transponders by requesting and observing a turn. If this results in a significant displacement from the planned track and vectors back are not forthcoming, pilots should ask. Indeed, in any situation in which pilots require assistance from ATC they should request it.

NOTES:

CLASS D AIRSPACE

CHIRP

Feb 2017, Issue 71

I took off with a passenger on a VFR flight in my flex wing microlight, planning to overfly the city (of Edinburgh), which lies within the CTR of Edinburgh Airport. This was a flight I had done a number of times. I am familiar with the airspace, confident using the radio and working with ATC and have an aircraft with a mode S transponder.

I received clearance from ATC for my preferred routing, not above 2000 ft, as expected. Unfortunately, shortly after entering the CTR it became clear that low cloud would mean we could not continue VFR, so we cut short the transit and left the CTR at our planned exit point. On exiting the CTR rather than return to the airfield early I decided we should fly south to my passenger's childhood home at Galashiels. This took us towards rising ground (up to 2000 ft) so I started to climb. I cancelled the Basic Service I was receiving from Edinburgh Approach and advised them I would contact Scottish Information. I retuned my radio, and called Scottish Information who told me that Edinburgh Approach had been on the phone and to call them as I had just infringed their airspace by climbing into the CTA at 3,500 ft. I descended immediately, then contacted Edinburgh Approach who gave me a Basic Service until I was well outside of their CTA. Following the flight I phoned the Tower to apologise, thoroughly embarrassed that I managed to make such an error.

Lessons Learned:

There are some obvious immediate lessons that I have learned from this experience:

1. The primary cause of the infringement was my failure to monitor my altitude and stop my climb. I had intended to climb to 3,000 ft, which would have been 500 ft below the TMA base. At the point I was informed of my infringement I had reached 3,800 ft.

2. The diversion to Galashiels was not planned, so I had an increased navigational workload in the cockpit to ensure I was on track and was concentrating on the lateral navigation rather than vertical. Though I am familiar with the airspace and have transited under the TMA many times before, on this occasion I didn't pick up the 3,500 ft floor of the TMA on my chart as something to watch out for in particular. In future I need to be extra careful when deviating from my flight plan and ensure I consider vertical navigation.

3. There was no need to change from Edinburgh Approach to Scottish Information at that particular point. This created a self-inflicted high workload for no benefit. Changing from Edinburgh to Scottish required about 2 minutes of concentration - listening for a gap, speaking, retuning, and changing squawk, then contacting Scottish. Plenty of time for an altitude deviation to develop. In future I will only change frequency when flying straight

and level. Given that I was still operating under the CTA, remaining with Edinburgh Approach would have been the better option. In other words: Aviate, Navigate, Communicate! Beyond this, there are a couple of other lessons learned.

4. While inside the CTR I had been paying attention to my altitude like a hawk to ensure that I remained below 2,000 ft. Leaving the CTR psychologically may have made me think that I was now out of Controlled Airspace and "released" from needing to pay particular attention to my altitude.

5. Having a transponder, and having told Edinburgh Approach my intentions to contact Scottish Information made it straightforward to resolve the infringement and minimise the impact. I habitually call for a Basic Service on anything other than the most local of flights, and will continue to do so.

6. As always, both Edinburgh Approach and Scottish Information were completely professional, and beyond Scottish Information informing me of my initial infringement it was not mentioned again. Nevertheless, it did cause quite some stress in the cockpit and my performance was impaired for at least 10 minutes afterwards. I have read in CHIRP FEEDBACK in the past that other pilots who have infringed airspace have experienced similar stress, particularly if asked to contact the tower following their flight (gulp!) or been admonished on the radio. I'm very grateful that neither of these things happened to me.

7. I hesitate to suggest what anyone else could have done to prevent something that was entirely my fault, but if Edinburgh Approach had asked if I could stay on their frequency until outside the CTA, I would have done so. I don't know if this would have prevented my infringement

but it would have reduced workload and kept me on an appropriate frequency if anything did occur.

CHIRP Comment: Thank you for this thorough report and comprehensive analysis. Many infringements result from high workload and therefore managing workload is highly desirable. It may not always be possible to wait until flying straight and level to change frequency but it makes sense to choose opportune moments for discretionary changes and other actions that draw upon one's available mental capacity. Using the Edinburgh listening squawk rather than switching to Scottish Information was an option. However, in the circumstances in which the reporter was already receiving a service from Edinburgh, he is correct in suggesting that it would have been better to have remained on the Edinburgh frequency until he was clear of the TMA. Of note, and notwithstanding the possible shortcomings of electronic Apps reported elsewhere in this Edition, an in-flight airspace App would have possibly saved the day. Once again, it was good to read about the professionalism of ATC and the lack of any admonishment over the radio.

NOTES:

NEAR INFRINGEMENT

CHIRP

Feb 2017, Issue 71

During a local VFR flight from [ ], my tablet's airspace App showed that the base of Controlled Airspace was FL55. I had climbed to 4600 ft on regional QNH of 1017 squawking mode C when I was informed that [ ] Approach had complained to them that I had infringed their Controlled Airspace. When I queried [the complaint, I was informed] that the base of Controlled Airspace was FL45, so I immediately descended. During the return to [ ] I was asked to phone [the controlling authority] after landing.

Upon landing, a comparison of the chart on my app with my paper ICAO chart confirmed that the App was missing airway [ ]. This airway has existed since long before this App was first released.

The conversation with the air traffic controller in [ ] was not at all unpleasant – he very much took the approach of it being a learning exercise for all involved. Because I had reached 4600 ft on 1017 I had actually avoided an infringement by about 10 ft (at 30 ft per hPa the difference between 1017 and 1013.25 is about 110 ft). He had been under the impression that I was flying higher than this because my transponder's altitude encoder had said so. My altitude encoder was at the time operating off cockpit pressure rather than static pressure (a plumbing fault that has since been rectified), which would account for the over-reading.

An email conversation with the makers of the App on my tablet proved interesting. After checking they confirmed that it was indeed missing [the airway], and they explained that all this data is not only entered by hand but that it needs a fair bit of tweaking to get all the airspace boundaries to align neatly. Up to now I had naively assumed that populating the database of such Apps was simply a matter of the manufacturers entering the published co-ordinates and that the software did the rest.

Lessons to take away:

1. Just as with general A to B navigation, do not rely on GPS charts as your primary means of airspace awareness. Use the ICAO chart as the primary source, and your App as a support aid. If you insist on using an App foremost in flight, check every bit of airspace on your route against the chart beforehand or on your own head be it if you infringe.

2. Do not depend upon the ATC service which you are in contact with to warn you of the possibility of infringing local Controlled Airspace, even if they do have SSR and you have mode C.

3. For those readers who spot that had I not been squawking mode C ATC would not have known of the apparent infringement and I would have avoided any possibility of incurring their wrath, remember that the main reason for using a transponder is the far more serious concern of collision avoidance. The displeasure of NATS is vastly preferable to an encounter with an Airbus A320 in its

native environment. In short, use every resource at your disposal, but be wary of their limitations.

CHIRP Comment: Official charts provide a definitive reference whereas 3rd party Apps must be used with caution. That said, the benefits of using electronic Apps far outweigh the possibility of shortcomings. Nevertheless, it is important to carry an up-to-date chart with the track annotated on it in case electronic devices fail in flight. Drawing the line on the chart provides an opportunity to familiarise oneself with the route and confirm it is clear of controlled airspace and other navigational hazards. We agree wholeheartedly with the reporter's remarks about value of squawking with altitude. Clearly, it is important to ensure that the altitude readout is accurate but the benefits of being conspicuous on ATC radars and the collision avoidance systems carried by other aircraft outweigh any other consideration. Finally, it was good to read that the conversation after the flight with the controller was conducted amicably and professionally.

NOTES:

DONCASTER INFRINGEMENT

CHIRP

Feb 2017, Issue 71

Presented with a "window of opportunity" during a period of family issues and commitments I recently planned to hire and fly a PA28 Cherokee from [ ] to Sandtoft. However on the morning of the flight I decided to request a change to the cheaper Cessna 150L.

I had already pre-planned the PA28 using Sky Demon GPS on a mini iPad which I now updated – I also routinely draw lines on a map and include printed data from Sky Demon. My mini iPad is an early version matched to a GNS 2000 blue-tooth device. Pre-flight, start-up and take-off were as normal and I set course for my first waypoint changing to London Information with no acknowledgement from [the departure airfield] Ground Radio.

Confirmed my first turn at Market Harborough with London Info when I realised that the GPS combination was not working, no quick solution so grab map and CRP1, find and confirm position and continue on - updating London at waypoints as requested. Approaching Gainsborough I requested descent from 3000 ft to 1500 ft in preparation for approach to Sandtoft and London advised me to squawk 7000 and free-call Doncaster Radar. Contact was made and as I approached the M180 I requested a frequency change to Sandtoft which was approved. Reception was intermittent but I eventually made contact with Sandtoft and requested joining and landing instructions. Reception was broken but I noted Runway 05 and the QFE. I could not see the airfield so called for clues getting no reply. By this time I realised that I had drifted further West than intended, nearing the M180/M18 junction to the North of Doncaster's Runway. Executing a sharp left 180 degree turn, tracking back along the M180, I called Sandtoft, who replied and at the same time picked up the airfield ahead. So requested approach from left base and landing on 05, parking up as requested.

Reporting to Control I was handed a message to ring Doncaster Radar, which I had expected, but was unable to talk to the Supervisor and having passed my details was advised that he would contact me in due course. The Controller at Sandtoft was concerned that I had not received his radio messages although he had heard all my transmissions. Analysing communications on the flight up to Sandtoft I noted that conversations between other traffic and London Information had seemed broken at times but appeared of no immediate concern to me – or had I missed something?

Having re-set the GPS, checked the radio, headset and connections the return trip was uneventful apart from the continued occasional intermittent reception. Subsequent discussion with our Flying School Staff revealed that other users had experienced similar occurrences. The aircraft is due for an electronic upgrade.

CHIRP Comment: Intermittent technical faults are often difficult to resolve but should be reported and recorded in the aircraft tech log in order that pilots are forewarned of potential problems before they fly. The reporter may have been distracted by the intermittent radio reception but the incident was caused by a navigational error despite him wisely carrying a paper chart to use when there were problems with the GPS. Sandtoft is on the edge of the Doncaster CTR and beneath the CTA which has a base of 1500 ft. Since the preferred join at Sandtoft is from the overhead at 1500 ft there is little room for error vertically and laterally, so particular care is required in planning. The reporter might also have been predisposed to an error through the family issues he reported. Pilots might usefully consider the acronym 'IMSAFE' before flight as a prompt to consider whether there are personal factors that might affect their performance: IMSAFE = Illness, Medication, Stress, Alcohol, Fatigue and Eating.

NOTES:

RADAR VECTORS TO APPROACH

CHIRP

Nov 2016, Issue 70

The ILS glideslope was unserviceable, as it had been the previous day.

The controller was clear that it was vectors to LOC/DME approach. I was vectored on to localiser at 2000 ft then handed off to [ ] Approach. The Approach Plate indicated a descent at 4 DME, but at 4.7 DME conditions were VMC and I could see the PAPIs showing 2 white and 2 red.

Momentary confusion, but then I realised that I was 200' above platform [initial approach altitude], so started descent 0.6 DME early and all was fine. However, in IMC I would not have had the cue of the PAPIs. My first warning would have been 200 ft high at 3 DME, requiring a rate of descent of 1000 fpm reduced to 600 fpm at 2 DME with a decision at about 1 DME, so far from a stabilised approach.

I am not blaming the extremely helpful controller, but I think that this underlines that controllers of ILS airfields may not get the practice of 2D (lateral guidance only)/Non-Precision Approaches (NPA).

I mentioned this on an online IFR forum and someone related exactly the same having happened to him recently at [a different airfield], so this is not a one-off or localised.

Lessons Learned:

ATCOs maybe need to be reminded, when the glideslope is unserviceable, of the importance of platform altitude on a NPA. Pilots may need to pay more attention to ensuring that they have been descended to platform, and requesting it otherwise.

CHIRP Comment: The Air Navigation Service Provider was grateful for the report which drew attention to some inconsistencies among controllers. Aircraft should be descended to the published platform so that the pilot can commence descent at the pre-briefed distance out from the airfield. The reporter is correct in reminding controllers and pilots of the importance of ensuring that the final approach commences from the correct initial approach altitude – neither above nor below.

NOTES:

AIRSPACE INFRINGEMENT

CHIRP

Aug 2016, Issue 69

I took what was intended to be a short VFR flight to maintain club currency as I realised that as I was going to have to travel abroad for a funeral of a close family member in a few days and my club currency would have run out. The conditions were good with good visibility throughout for my short flight over an area well known to me. Unfortunately, shortly into my flight the detachable lead from my headset snagged the harness and pulled out of the ear cup leaving me distracted by the lack of radio communication. I sought to rectify the problem not realising that the lead had become detached and while trying to sort out the problem I found myself monitoring the wrong altimeter. Quite how or why I do not know except perhaps the fact that subconsciously my attention was not where it should have been having suffered two close family bereavements in a relatively short space of time. While I felt fine it seems the relatively minor issue of the headset cable working lose and my efforts to rectify the problem became a major distraction which led me to believe I was flying below the TMA when in fact I had inadvertently entered it.

When I sorted out the problem with the radio I became aware that there had been an airspace infringement in the area I was flying as a result of a message between the tower and another aircraft. I hadn't immediately appreciated it was my infringement as to all intents and purposes the reading I had on the altimeter I was monitoring was showing me below the TMA. I decided to return to the airfield and then realised that I had the wrong altimeter setting in the subscale.

When on the ground I called the tower to explain the situation. I recognised that I had made a mistake and while I felt pretty stupid I knew I had to hold my hand up to it. Thankfully [ ] Radar were satisfied a genuine mistake had been made and the matter could be put to one side, for which I am eternally grateful.

Lessons Learned:

I have learned the valuable lesson that one really has to be strict with oneself when deciding whether it is wise to fly. While I hadn't appreciated that I was probably under stress as a result of the recent bereavement, the second one in a few months, I allowed those factors to distract me from my instrument management when a small problem developed in the cockpit.

I have also learned that it would be wise in the future to set both altimeters to the same subscale if I do not need to monitor two different pressure settings so that if a distraction occurs I am not mislead by erroneous information.

I have also decided that my [ ], while a nice headset, are not to be used when acting as Pilot in Command as the lead is prone to pull out of the ear cup if it gets caught on the harness.

I still feel pretty stupid though for allowing myself to have got into that situation.

CHIRP Comment: We all make mistakes because we are human but we should only feel embarrassed if we don't learn from them; therefore we are grateful to this reporter for sharing his experience. There are many ways of using 2 altimeters: both to the same setting; one on QFE, the other on QNH; or if climbing above the TA, the main on 1013 and the standby on QNH. It is important to develop Standard Operating Procedures so that we know automatically what each one is telling us in any circumstance.

Distraction is a trap that awaits even the most wary and pilots are more susceptible to it when they are not fully focused on the task in hand. It can be very difficult to assess one's own fitness to fly after illness or following a psychological upset such as bereavement, redundancy, divorce etc. Given this difficulty it is essential to err on the safe side when making the judgment. Finally, minimise the potential for physical distraction; if personal equipment is unsuitable for some reason, it needs to be remedied or replaced.

NOTES:

DANGER AREA INFRINGEMENT

CHIRP

Aug 2016, Issue 69

I flew through a live danger area despite having checked NOTAMs, because I mis-read the activation date on the NOTAM. UK dates are normally by convention DD/MM/YY, but NOTAMs use YY/MM/DD on the notoriously poor AIS.org website. This led to me reading '16/03/20' as 16th March (i.e. last Wednesday) when I scanned the NOTAMs at 06:30 on a Sunday morning ready for an early flight down to west Wales, when I was half asleep. As a result, I twice flew straight through the middle of D[ ] when it was live on Sunday 20/03/16, without a second thought since it is normally Mon-Fri operation only. Luckily, the range controller's lookouts were wide-awake, saw me in the very bad haze, and suspended operations. Very embarrassing, and could easily have been much worse.

Lessons Learned:

It would be REALLY helpful if NOTAMs on AIS.org could show dates in the conventional UK format. One of the things we have to learn as pilots is human factors, and making information hard to readily understand is something which would raise a big red flag in that subject, so it's hard to understand why NATS have chosen to use such an inappropriate date format. I also know I am not alone in making this mistake, as the national range controller for the company who operate this range told me when I phoned to apologise. Ironically, if I had checked NOTAMs on virtually any other source than the official NATS-approved one, it would have shown the date in the normal UK format, and I wouldn't have been misled... Come on guys - sort it out! Everybody else has.

Lesson for me - check and double check. If you see a NOTAM for an area which could affect your flight, make doubly sure you have correctly read and understood it.

CHIRP Comment: The reporter is correct that the date format used for NOTAMs is open to misinterpretation. However it is a mathematically logical ISO standard adopted by ICAO and used worldwide in all NOTAMs, SNOWTAMs, ASHTAMs, information bulletins etc. Although it could be done, changing the format on the AIS website away from the ICAO standard risks causing greater confusion, particularly for foreign aviators and the large number of commercial users who systematically process the data by utilising the standard format. Without a great deal more evidence a change is highly unlikely. It should be noted that when using the AIS website, all of the NOTAMs that appear for a selected date will be relevant for that date.

NOTES:

PRESSURE FROM ATCO

CHIRP

May 2016, Issue 68

Experienced PPL training for IMC rating in own aircraft. Called to join for booked training slot at []. Told to remain well clear to south-west until slot time. Carried out holds at 3500 ft 10 NM south-west in clear airspace. ATC requested ETA for the beacon; student misread watch and stated time 5 mins in error, implying one minute to go. ATC responded with admonition that we were told to hold well clear (we were actually 10 miles clear). Instructed to climb to 5000 ft and proceed to beacon. During tear-drop entry to the hold, instructed to descend to 2500 ft. Whilst descending, turning, configuring the aircraft, consulting approach plate, ATC gave clearance for NDB approach. Heavily loaded student omitted 3 words from read-back; aggressive reply from ATCO repeating clearance; student even more loaded by admonition and still performing complex flying task again read back incomplete response, triggering sharp response from ATC. As we approached the beacon in the hold, ATC cleared us for the procedure which the student understandably began (without calling beacon outbound). ATC then advised clear for the approach next time round the hold, when we were already established on the approach. At this point I abandoned the exercise for return to base (we were VMC throughout). Final aggression from ATC - I called leaving the frequency and ATC insisted on knowing who we would call. Good VMC so I intended to call nobody but use listening squawk; in Class G airspace you don't have to speak to anybody!

Lessons Learned:

ATCO demonstrated no understanding of the high workload and pressures in the cockpit, and the associated human limitations. Student was technically in error, but matters were compounded by the critical and admonitory tone of the ATCO. It is the instructor's role to pick up and correct the errors; R/T slips should be publicly corrected only if there is a risk to flight safety.

CHIRP Comment: Unlike Information or Instructions, ATCOs have no discretion with Clearances; they have to be read back verbatim. In this incident it appears that both the pilots and controller were working hard and, given the routine difficulty of knowing how busy a pilot or controller might be at any particular moment, it is vital that pilots and controllers should use clearly-enunciated standard phraseology with no hint of emotion, frustration or disapproval. There is no requirement for pilots in Class G airspace to declare their next intended frequency but it can be helpful for controllers to know in some circumstances. When there is no intended frequency the expression "going/switching en route" can be used - or for traditionalists the following was heard a few years ago, "I am heading north and switching off my wireless!"

NOTES:

VISUAL FLIGHT RULES
CHIRP

May 2016, Issue 68

I was engaged on an instructional cross country flight with a TAF at my destination [in Class D airspace] of 'EG** 2112/2118 21013KT 9999 FEW012 TEMPO 21122118 21018G30KT 6000 RA BKN 008'. The flight went very well and the student learnt a great deal due to the strength of the wind and commented on the high ground speed and the need to keep ahead of the navigation. He carried out all radio calls and handled the aircraft throughout.

Approximately 10 NM from [our destination] the student called and was surprised to hear we could not join as the visibility was less than 5kms! We had good ground contact and the visibility was between 3 and 5kms. I advised we would continue and assess the situation from closer in. The student was still flying the aircraft, as the forecast stated TEMPO, I felt that this was a passing shower and would clear, allowing for our relatively low ground speed we had a little time to pass.

Some 3 miles from the airfield, still at 1400' and with good ground contact and the student still flying the aircraft, we were again told we could not join as the visibility was less than 5000 metres. I confirmed I had good ground contact and was happy to continue, this request was refused. I had no option other than divert.

I tried an airfield downwind but they were water logged, so the next option was [ ], although it is considerably higher field elevation than our planned destination. ATC at [ ] were as ever excellent and initially offered a downwind join. However, due to deteriorating weather we were forced to climb and eventually landed uneventfully from an ILS. The wind was quite strong so when the hangar was offered I accepted. Shame the total bill came to £243.00 with the taxi as [ ] do not accept weather diversions!

Lessons Learned:

I have been instructing for many years and have always believed that the pilot has ultimate responsibility for the safe conduct of the flight, taking into account available weather information and any ATC observations. Now it seems that an airfield in class D airspace can just close. The major concern I have is that SERA states:

> "It does not matter what the pilot can see it is the official aerodrome meteorological report that determines if flights can take place. When two visibility values are reported the lower value is used."

Surely there should be an element of common sense. When the controller is fully aware of the pilot's ability, as some months earlier I had landed in much worst conditions.

CHIRP Comment: The reporter is correct that it is the SERA regulations that have reduced the minima to be applied for VFR flight in control zones. SERA.5005 Visual flight rules states:

(b) Except when a special VFR clearance is obtained from an air traffic control unit, VFR flights shall not take off or land at an aerodrome within a control zone, or enter the aerodrome traffic zone or aerodrome traffic circuit when the reported meteorological conditions at that aerodrome are below the following minima:

1. the ceiling is less than 450 m (1 500 ft); or
2. the ground visibility is less than 5km.

This aerodrome is equipped with cloud base and visibility measuring equipment. The controller had no other option when he advised the reporter that he could not join the circuit because the weather (4000m, few at 900 ft and broken at 1500 ft) was below VFR minima for arrivals and departures. The aerodrome was not closed and would have been available for use in an emergency. However, this was not an emergency situation as the instructor was always fully in control of a serviceable aircraft and at no stage was his situational awareness compromised, including his options for a diversion. The incident also demonstrates the importance in poor weather flight planning of identifying a diversion airfield with weather that is forecast to be suitable for the duration of the flight.

NOTES:

INFRINGEMENT OF CLASS D ZONE

CHIRP

Aug 2015, Issue 65

Yesterday as the instructor i/c I infringed the class D airspace at [ ]. How did I allow this to happen and what could I have done to prevent it? The purpose of the flight was to give the newly qualified PPL, who had learned to fly at a non-radio site, experience talking to controllers. I felt we had planned very thoroughly - meeting the day before the flight to plan, which included calling [ ] to discuss the most convenient level for us to transit and even looking at landmarks on Google Earth. The outbound flight went well transiting the Zone (the controller was clearly busy but went out of his way to accommodate our non transponder equipped aircraft). Over extended coffee at [land away airfield] we planned the return to our departure airfield. My student wanted the way back to be 'lighter' on the radio work and so we planned a route that would be outside CAS but parallel the boundary of the Class D. Nevertheless I insisted that we still get a Basic Service from the LARS frequency as I believe that contact with relevant controllers always enhances safety – as it happened this was my one good decision. The first half of the leg which mirrored the zone boundary about 3 miles distant went perfectly so much so that the handling pilot could not see the mid-point ground feature so I did a very steep 360 turn to let her see what was below the aircraft and then let her continue on heading. Knowing we were close to the boundary I monitored the DI carefully and she stayed on heading. I had just started to think we were a little off track but discounted the evidence of my eyes as P1/S had been keeping a constant heading (which had worked-out so well thus far). Things then started happening quickly, the [aircraft] we had been watching on our left was turning right towards us (about 8 miles – similar level), and the controller called us telling us we had strayed into the zone (about one mile) and turned us right. Throughout the flight and once home, I kept trying unsuccessfully to understand how it could have happened. Finally it has 'dawned'; I now believe the very steep 360 orbit over the mid-point took the DI out of sync and so even though P1/S appeared to maintain heading we were in fact flying left of track.

Lessons Learned:

The return flight is worthy of as much detailed planning as the outbound and I should not have planned a route with such a small margin of safety from the zone boundary. It would have been wise to have had a fool-proof way of monitoring proximity to the boundary (for example saying, 'I must always have a specific feature e.g. road /railway on my left') and as soon as I suspected we were drifting north, knowing how close I was to the boundary, I should have acted. Finally to check /re set the DI after any extreme manoeuvre. I am now buying a NATS AWARE GPS set.

CHIRP Comment: The reporter has said it all. Thank you.

NOTES:

INFRINGEMENT OF CAS

CHIRP

Feb 2014, Issue 59

During one of the best flying days I've ever experienced I undertook what was to be my most ambitious flight in my 8 years of flying. The journey was to be solo outbound [from Kent to the NW] and returning the same day with 2 passengers; the round trip would be 530 NM and almost 5.5 hours total. The outbound journey was completed without incident and was certainly one of the most satisfying flights I've had to date. On the return I had planned to climb to 5000 ft and to maintain this level until after overflying Oxford. I then intended to descend to 2400 ft to remain under the London TMA and to remain at this height until descending into the circuit at my destination. However, sometime after passing BOV I encountered some strong thermal activity, which increased my height to around 2700 ft. Having noticed this I carried out an immediate descent to 2400 ft again. After a few minutes I was aware that I had again gained height and was once again in the TMA. My passenger in the right hand seat who is a non-flyer asked what the issue was and as he was holding the chart for me I tried to explain to him the legend depicting the airspace above us. Between the two of us we concluded that the TMA at this point was 3500 ft not 2500 ft after all. Stupid mistake as I've flown this part of the route many times in the past and know well that it's 2500 ft. I therefore decided that I needn't worry and continued at around 2600-2700 ft. On contacting Southend Radar just south of Stapleford I was asked my altitude and reported 2600 ft. The controller advised an immediate descent to 2400 ft which I did. Clearly I had been infringing the London TMA for quite some time. The rest of the flight was uneventful.

Lessons Learned:

Having now had time to review the whole incident I have made the following observations. In spite of having planned the flight thoroughly I failed to follow my planning to a sufficient degree. What caused the infringement? Well the strong thermal activity certainly caused the increase in altitude I experienced but that's not an excuse, just a reason. Why did I not control this? A couple of factors come to mind, firstly this happened after having flown for some 4.5 hours in one day, by far the most I've ever done and I'm sure that tiredness played a significant part. Secondly, after flying at or above 5000 ft for around 1.5 hours somehow the ground seemed ever so close when at 2400 ft. This may have led to a psychological feeling of being too low. What will I do to avoid this in future? When marking my route on my chart in future I now plan to mark each of the legs with the maximum altitude permissible for that leg. Had I done this on this occasion there would have been no doubt about what level the TMA began. It is also worth noting that this phase of my flight was the only time I was not actually in contact with an ATC unit, having signed off from Oxford stating I would be free calling Southend. Stapleford was closed for the day. My aircraft carries Mode S, which I always use and had I been in touch with London Info or Essex Radar, they may well have been able to warn me of the infringement much earlier. Although I was listening to Southend they were not aware of my presence until I called them south of Stapleford. In future I will remain in contact with someone at all times, or at least make use of the increasing number of listening squawks available. I have been flying now for some 8 years and believe this is the first time I've been the cause of a major infringement. This does not sit well with me and hope that the experience will sharpen my flying in the future.

CHIRP Comment: The reporter has honestly and correctly identified important lessons and factors to remind other pilots about some of the principal causes of infringements. Key elements were flight planning the route only 100 ft below the base of the TMA in weather conditions conducive to thermal activity, compounded by incorrectly interpreting the base of the TMA from the aeronautical chart. Recently announced changes to the 1:500k and 1:250k VFR charts may assist with this latter issue; see the NATS AIS website for details: www.nats-uk.eadit.com.

Another factor may have been the distraction of seeking the assistance of a non-flyer passenger, particularly given the complexity of the airspace depicted on the chart. Finally, it would have been sensible to call Farnborough LARS for the transit beneath the TMA.

NOTES:

INADVERTENT CLIMB
CHIRP

Feb 2014, Issue 59

On an instructional flight, with an experienced and competent student (a PPL holder regaining currency), we had planned a visual navigation exercise, which would take us right to the edge of the Gatwick CTA at 1400 ft (an altitude chosen to prevent an infringement of the CTA if we should slightly overshoot our turning point).

The student was PF, and we had turned as planned at Bough Beech Reservoir. We had planned a climb to 2400 ft for this leg but I elected to remain at 1400 ft initially rather than starting our climb immediately, in order to satisfy myself that we were definitely well clear of the Gatwick CTA before climbing.

Having climbed to 2400 ft, at the halfway point of the leg, we fixed our position as halfway between Crowborough and Wadhurst. I asked the student to give me our corrected heading to track to Hastings Pier, which he did. Shortly after we turned to the new heading and while we were revising our ETA, Farnborough Radar called to advise us to descend immediately. Our altimeter showed we had inadvertently climbed to 2600 ft. I had allowed myself to become distracted by our navigation corrections, to the detriment of keeping a watchful eye on our altitude.

I believe that having just left the vicinity of the Gatwick CTA, where I had been acutely aware of the risk of infringing, I had allowed myself to relax too much and neglected to give the proper attention to other CAS in the vicinity. I am very grateful to the Farnborough LARS ATCO for their watchful eye and prompt action, which likely prevented us climbing even further into CAS.

Lessons Learned:

1. As an inexperienced instructor, with a competent and capable student, I believe I had allowed myself to become too much of an equal partner in the conduct of the flight, rather than remaining aware of my responsibility as PIC. I let the student's competence lull me into a false sense of security. I learned that I am PIC of an instructional flight, no matter how competent and capable the student, and that I must remain vigilant and on-guard against errors and distractions.

2. After leaving the immediate vicinity of the Gatwick CTA, I had just been working hard to ensure we did not infringe airspace. I believe when we tracked away from Gatwick, I relaxed, feeling that the high-risk time for an infringement had now passed, and that this complacency contributed significantly to my lack of awareness of other airspace we might infringe. The lesson learned is that if I catch myself relaxing and feeling that danger has now passed, this is exactly the time I need to be most on-guard.

3. The ATCO at Farnborough Radar doubtless prevented an even more serious infringement. I will be emphasising to students the value of LARS as another point at which

the error chain can be broken to minimise the consequences of a lapse in concentration.

CHIRP Comment: Another honest account rich in lessons for others. This was another case in which pilot-in-command, an instructor, had elected to fly only 100 ft below the base of the London TMA and then inadvertently climbed into controlled airspace. Fortunately in this occurrence the instructor had mitigated his risks by utilising an ATS from Farnborough.

NOTES:

CLASS G AIRSPACE

CHIRP

Nov 2013, Issue 58

I wish to respond to the "Instrument Approaches in Class 'G' Airspace" report in the latest FEEDBACK. Class 'G' airspace is free to all users at the moment and I would suggest the approaches in it have to be flown at the pilot's own risk while maintaining separation from other traffic by lookout or radar service.

For example, the GNSS approach for Shoreham Airport commences at 2200 feet, from the west just north of Parham gliding site and from the east just north of Ringmer gliding site and is not shown on charts likely to be used by non-instrument rated pilots. The base of the London TMA in this area is 2500 feet, it is also an extremely busy corridor for light aircraft transiting east west around the Gatwick zone, gliders and hang gliders/paragliders from the various South Downs Launch sites, and yes they do get into the instrument approach area on thermic days.

Is it reasonable to expect all other traffic to avoid the airspace south of the Gatwick zone in case someone wants to make an instrument approach to Shoreham? Many light aircraft are probably only there to avoid the Farnborough bottleneck.

CHIRP Comment: The report raises an important issue relating to the awareness of GA pilots to the existence of a GNSS approach procedure, particularly in cases where these were established at airfields with either a FIS or an Air/Ground Service.

Although GNSS final approach paths should be adequately annotated on aeronautical charts by a fan/cone symbol, there is currently no provision for the let-down pattern to be depicted. GNSS approaches are promulgated in the UK AIP in the same manner as other instrument approaches. If you are flying in the vicinity of an airfield that you know has an instrument approach procedure, it is good airmanship to call ATC on the RT to make yourself known and to learn the whereabouts of any traffic in the instrument pattern.

NOTES:

CHAPTER 7
NEAR MISS & SEPARATION

"A little mountain will kill you just as dead as a big one if you fly into it."
Stephen Coonts

BENEFITS OF LISTENING SQUAWK

CHIRP

Feb 2017, Issue 71

Flying west into sun on a good VFR evening, my intention was to route over Bovingdon, Tring, past RAF Halton, and out to Waddesdon Manor (NW of Aylesbury) and return.

I only tend to fly with map and planning, rather than iPad inflight systems. I folded my current 1/4mil so Enfield Hertford was East, and Stevenage Leighton Buzzard at the Top, Heathrow south, which fitted the route nicely. Lines plotted.

Conscious of the proximity of Luton, and complicated airspace to West, I elected to set 0013 and monitor 129.55 shortly after departure, per listening squawks. Approaching Cheddington airfield, I noted Ivinghoe Beacon (spot height marked on map 817) and noted, as my folded map showed, that the CTR at the surface would remain South if I diverted from my plans and routed direct from Cheddington to the Dunstable 'Lion', for my passenger's sightseeing benefit, then turned round and came back again to Cheddington, before continuing on my original plan to Aylesbury. I even pointed out to my passenger that the map showed this.

I turned East and moments later I heard my callsign on the frequency from Luton's controller. I replied. He asked my intentions and said that I was entering (or had entered, I forget in the heat of it) Controlled Airspace, and that I was to turn North West immediately. I did. Luton were using RW26 and I was 10 miles approximately West, so well away from the 'action'. Actually I was very startled by what I'd done and I wasn't sure how I could have done it. I reversed course and returned to base without completing my flight to my final turning point

Lessons Learned:

Listening squawk was a saviour. I guess I was being monitored and I was called as soon as I was heading their way. Where I'd folded my map, the CTR D lettering over the centre of Luton town, was exactly on my fold and was overlooked. Looking at the Airspace boxes around Tring and Dunstable which are complex, I noted that I was close to but north of the CTR, starting at SFC level and below the box over Dunstable which I read as starting at 3500. I "assumed" that gliders would operate in clear Airspace, up to 3500.

Even looking at this small slice of airspace over Dunstable now, in my lounge, it's still not really immediately clear where the Airspace is. I can see a very light pink shading in this box but also the bold CTR D SFC 3500 with the arrow pointing to it from BNN VOR leading me to believe that I was outside the surface restriction. I probably saw what I wanted to see but I think the map design made it worse. The bright ambient sun necessitating sunglasses, probably concealed the light pink hue. I diverted from my original route, albeit briefly, which was clearly unwise even in excellent VMC. I knew exactly where I was and I thought I was being good but I think it's a mistake that others could easily make because I was where I shouldn't have been. It worried me even on the return leg of the flight and I hope I wasn't diverted from my primary task of flying safely but honestly I was unnerved by it (am I ashamed to say?). No, I will learn from it. I'll never do it again and the listening squawk certainly helped save anything further.

Apologies to Luton, they probably get this all the time.

CHIRP Comment: We are grateful for this report. Unfortunately Controlled Airspace is often infringed. In the 2 months from mid-Nov 16 to mid-Jan 17 NATS recorded 59 airspace infringements with 2 losses of separation from commercial air traffic. It is also unfortunate that there is no such thing as a minor infringement. Any uncleared entry into Controlled Airspace can cause disruption and delays to the flow of traffic and the removal of controllers from their consoles while they file a report; depending upon the circumstances, controllers can be unavailable for the remainder of their shift. As noted in the editorial, ad hoc free navigation can result in infringements and mistakes can be very distracting even when, as in this case, ATC have made a good save. The reporter is right to temper his embarrassment with the knowledge that he has learned from the incident and shared his experience. Does anyone doubt the value of listening squawks?

NOTES:

GLIDER IN PROXIMITY TO CLOUD

CHIRP

Feb 2017, Issue 71

I was routing down from [ ] to [ ] at FL060 on an IFR flight plan. My route was one I had done before: [ ] - Aberdeen - Newcastle - Durham - Linton - Cranwell - BKY – [ ]

I was receiving a Deconfliction Service from Durham as I was 90% IMC at my level with heavy rain showers and broken (7 OKTAS) cumulus. At the time in question I popped out of IMC into a "hole" in the clouds and to my 11 o'clock at 1/2 a mile was a glider circling in the hole in the clouds at the same level. Durham had no contact with this glider on their Radar at all as I asked. I asked for and was granted an immediate 70 degree right turn until it was felt I was clear of the traffic, when I was then released back on track.

Had the glider been 1/2 mile to the right then I would almost certainly have hit it. It was flying in what "it" felt were VMC conditions totally oblivious to the fact that other aircraft were flying in straight lines, not circling, through IMC conditions. As it is a lightweight aircraft it did not paint on radar.

Lessons Learned:

The lesson to me was that even in IFR flight there is always the unexpected. A suggestion to avoid this in the future is twofold:

1. Gliders MUST always be aware that if they are surrounded by cloud towers then although they might be in VMC, the aircraft around them will be in IMC flying in straight lines from point A to point B passing from cloud to cloud and thus WILL NOT see them until it is too late.
2. Like Yachts, Gliders cannot easily be seen on radar and therefore need to augment their ability to be visible on a compulsory basis, either using radar reflectors aka yachts or with transponders so that at least something is reflected back to the ground that they are there.

It was only by chance that this glider did not have another aircraft hit it, the hole it was circling in was not that big.

CHIRP Comment: Gliders can be encountered anywhere in UK Class G airspace up to FL195. They are hard to see and don't reliably paint on ATC radars. In Class G airspace all pilots share an equal responsibility to avoid collisions. Powered aircraft are required to give way to gliders except when approaching head on, or approximately so, and there is a danger of collision; in this case both aircraft shall turn to the right. These responsibilities apply equally to flights under VFR and IFR. The reporter had sensibly agreed a Deconfliction Service for his IFR flight in IMC but the glider did not provide sufficient radar returns for ATC to alert him to its presence. Unless some form of electronic conspicuity is fitted the only reliable way of avoiding gliders is to see them. Therefore when operating under VFR pilots (both Power AND Glider) must observe the appropriate rules for separation from cloud (for flight above 3000 ft: 1500 m horizontally and 300 m (1000 ft) vertically clear of cloud) in order that they can see and be seen. The fitting of appropriate electronic conspicuity devices to gliders and powered aircraft is strongly encouraged.

NOTES:

WAS IT AN INCURSION?

CHIRP

Aug 2016, Issue 69

I would genuinely like an answer to the question whether, in the circumstances I am describing, I would technically have been guilty of a runway incursion offence.

Having re-joined the circuit I was instructed by ATC after the downwind call to turn onto right base, but warned that I might have to go around because I was Number Two to land and there was a business jet just ahead on the ILS. Just as I started to turn and reduce the throttle the controller cancelled his last instruction and told me to orbit left from my present position, which I did (with a slight correction to take me to the more orthodox orbiting area where I had orbited many times).

After one orbit he told me for the second time I could proceed to base, and as I began my descent I saw the business jet reach the runway threshold. After I turned on to the centreline and reported Final I was instructed to "continue approach", which I read back. As I neared the threshold I could see the jet taxying on the runway about 1000 metres away (its total length is about 1800m), so there was no danger of my catching him before he turned off; but I had still not been cleared to land and was debating with myself what to do. Should I go around?

The "clear to land" call from ATC came about ten seconds or less (I would estimate 5 but I was too busy to count) before I crossed the threshold.

Would I have been guilty of a serious infraction or only a minor technical one - or none at all - if I had presumed I was clear to land and had landed without being given explicit permission to do so, based on my appraisal of the situation which I could plainly see? I vacated the runway myself onto a left-hand taxiway about 300 metres beyond the threshold.

Should I have landed without final clearance to land (presuming that to be ATC's obvious intention), and what would have happened had I done so?

I don't feel particularly aggrieved about the incident as I have learnt that a certain degree of give and take smooths the relationship between pilots and controllers, and we all make mistakes.

CHIRP Comment: As noted earlier, a runway incursion is an event and not an offence, but the answer to the question is yes; if the aircraft had landed without a landing clearance being issued and acknowledged, a runway incursion would have occurred. "Continue approach and expect a late landing clearance" is occasionally used and might have been helpful in the reported circumstances. Landing without a clearance is not necessarily wrong depending upon the circumstances but it is an event that requires the submission of a Mandatory Occurrence Report to the CAA; the onus would be on the pilot to explain why he had landed without being cleared.

From CAP413 Radio Telephony Manual:
  4.56 The controller may or may not explain why the

landing clearance has been delayed but the instruction to 'continue' IS NOT an invitation to land and the pilot must wait for landing clearance or initiate a missed approach.

At some airfields the term 'land after' may be used as in, "call sign: land after the [aircraft type] ahead".

From CAP 413 again:

4.57 A landing aircraft may be permitted to touch down before a preceding landing aircraft has vacated the runway provided that:

1. The runway is long enough to allow safe separation between the two aircraft and there is no evidence to indicate that braking may be adversely affected;

2. It is during daylight hours;

3. The preceding landing aircraft is not required to backtrack in order to vacate the runway;

4. The controller is satisfied that the landing aircraft will be able to see the preceding aircraft which has landed, clearly and continuously, until it has vacated the runway; and

5. The pilot of the following aircraft is warned. (Responsibility for ensuring adequate separation rests with the pilot of the following aircraft.

Note that the word 'cleared' is not used because the pilot is responsible for separation from the aircraft ahead. Where aircraft performance differs markedly or where novice pilots are operating, controllers must be more cautious. Generally, if you haven't been cleared to land or instructed to 'land after' you must go around.

Some flying clubs impose a 'decision height' or range at which pilots should go around if not cleared by ATC or judged safe to continue by the pilot; 200 ft is a typical and safe decision gate for airfields with full ATC, FIS or Air/Ground Services. However, at events such as the LAA rally a 200 ft decision height would result in an unacceptable number of go-arounds. Ultimately, for VFR traffic in the absence of orders imposed by a club or school the decision is the pilot's to make. It should reflect the pilot's experience, the type of aircraft and the conditions – and at an airfield with ATC not be left so late that the wheels touch the ground as this would technically constitute a runway incursion.

NOTES:

NAVIGATION INCIDENT

CHIRP

Feb 2016, Issue 67

The incident was caused whilst flying the last leg of a VFR flight to Barton airfield (EGCB). I requested a frequency change from Liverpool 119.85 to Barton 120.25 on reaching the VRP junction M6/M58 (J26). I was squawking 7000 mode Charlie once released by Liverpool.

The direct track (114 degrees) from (J26 M6) to Barton - 12 miles - clips the North east corner of the low level corridor (maximum altitude 1300 ft) virtually overhead VRP Leigh Flash.

It has always been my practice not to fly direct to Barton from (J26 M6) but to remain at altitude 1800 ft and to take up a more Easterly track to clear the Northern and Eastern boundaries of the low level corridor before turning South and joining overhead at Barton. I consider this practice to be a safer option than descending to altitude 1300 ft for a short period of time and above a populated area before having to climb back to 1800 ft for the Barton overhead. I am familiar with the area and would normally have no problem remaining clear of the corridor simply from visual ground references.

On this occasion, and once in sight of Barton, I realised that I had not got the turn from the (J26 M6) correct since I was approaching Barton on a South Easterly heading and not Southerly which I was expecting, i.e. I was further West and therefore closer to the corridor than I should have been. The low level corridor and all surrounding airspace are clearly delineated on the 1/500,000 chart and associated altitudes are also clearly shown; there were no problems with VMC throughout the days flying.

I would like to make one mitigating comment, not an excuse but simply a possible contributing factor leading to my error. During the VFR flight, the direction indicator had become permanently caged (locked) and I completed the flight using the compass; I reported this problem on landing. It is generally accepted that flying on the much less damped compass is more difficult and requires more concentration than when using the DI. It may be that having to concentrate on the compass, which is positioned at a high level compared to the DI, distracted me a little from recognising the well-known landmarks of Wigan, Leigh and Leigh Flash; all of which I know well and observe in order to remain clear of the corridor once having made the turn from (J26 M6).

I do appreciate the importance of accurate navigation, including airspace altitude parameters, and I know that this becomes even more important when in close proximity to major international airports.

I really regret my error which led to the incident and I will take all the steps necessary to ensure no such problems occur in the future including;

Specific to this incident;

A) Flying 090 degrees from (J26) for 11 miles before turning south for Barton.

B) Not fly too close to the permitted altitude limits for the relevant airspace.

C) To squawk 7366 which is the Manchester conspicuity code and to monitor 118.575 when close to Manchester controlled airspace.

Generally;

A) Always squawk conspicuity codes whenever they are available and to monitor the relevant frequencies.

B) To become more familiar with navigating using the compass as opposed to the DI.

CHIRP Comment: We are grateful for this honest report and the reporter's identification of the steps we would also recommend for preventing similar problems in the future. The suggestion about practising navigation with compass alone is definitely worth trying; however, plan it carefully and ideally have a colleague along to act as a safety navigator, perhaps with a GPS set to monitor.

NOTES:

RUNWAY INCURSION

CHIRP

Feb 2016, Issue 67

As I approached the airport I was asked to do a standard overhead join and descend dead side. This I did and crossed over into the circuit on the crosswind end of the runway between 850 ft and 1,000 ft. As I approached the crosswind leg a twin engine aircraft was given take-off clearance and to advise my position I called that I was entering crosswind. There was no acknowledgement and the takeoff aircraft continued its take-off passing below my aircraft. I called the tower to advise that I was entering downwind and the tower replied and asked my altitude which I reported as 850 ft at the time. I was then told that I was number two to land on runway 27. As I turned base leg I called again and was told to follow the number one to land aircraft, which was a Cessna on final and I was asked to call final. As I turned final I called "turning final" and did not hear a response from the tower. On final approach I called "final contact one ahead'" I did not hear a reply but I was concentrating on the Cessna which had landed and was accelerating for a touch and go. I was on short final as the Cessna lifted and I continued to land. As I rolled onto the runway

I was asked to exit at C1 and after that I was given taxi instructions to the apron.

On paying my landing fee I was asked to talk with the tower who informed me that they had not heard any of my calls on final and although they had told me to follow the Cessna and told me that I was number two to the Cessna I had not been given formal landing permission and so my landing was a runway incursion.

I could not understand why they had not heard my transmissions of finals since they heard me after I landed and gave me taxi instructions.

After I departed I subsequently had problems contacting London information and found that my com 1 radio was intermittently failing to transmit even though the TX indicator was showing. Shortly after that the intermittent radio fault became continuous and I had to use com 2 for the rest of the flight.

I realise now that I landed without formal permission and this was due to the intermittent radio fault though I accept that it was my fault because I was concentrating on the aircraft that was going around to ensure that it was climbing away before I touched down.

Lessons Learned:

The lesson that I learned was not to be too distracted with watching other aircraft movements and thus not realise that I had not yet received formal landing clearance.

I also learned that I should not assume that the failure of ATC to respond was because they were busy but that they might not have heard my calls.

I also learned that even though the TX light of a com radio may indicate that it is transmitting it may not actually be transmitting. I was misled by this because the radio did not totally fail since it was still receiving and I could hear other aircraft on frequency which led me to believe the radio was working normally.

CHIRP Comment: A landing without clearance is technically a runway incursion and the subject of a Mandatory Occurrence Report.

> *Runway Incursion*: Any occurrence at an aerodrome involving the incorrect presence of an aircraft, vehicle or person on the protected area of a surface designated for the landing and take-off of aircraft.

That said, we have some sympathy with the reporter. Although he should have been suspicious when he did not receive an acknowledgement from ATC for the second time, he had already established 2-way contact before suffering this insidious RT failure at a critical point in the flight. The bottom line, as the reporter correctly identifies in his lessons learned, is that the only reliable way of knowing that a message has been successfully transmitted is when it provokes a response.

NOTES:

OVERHEAD JOIN

CHIRP

Feb 2014, Issue 59

I had a near miss last year on a 2000 ft overhead join. I'd heard the pilot saying he was passing overhead the airfield (no height offered), but I had a very long way to go before I called my overhead approach. We were both on radio, so I should have confirmed he was long gone. You mentioned last month a current Working Group on circuits. Is there a minimum height, of say 2500 ft, above a runway that is formally recommended for transiting planes who like to route flights using runways as their waypoints and a recommendation that airfields request that minimum clearance outside their zone when radioed? It seems unnecessary for the increase in GPS routing and circuit patterns to bring aircraft together at an exact height & at an exact place.

CHIRP Comment: There is no margin stipulated for flying above a traffic pattern but if there is sufficient useable airspace above, good airmanship, common sense and self-preservation all necessitate allowing sufficient height to avoid conflicts and/or discomforting other pilots. Don't forget that visual traffic patterns are based on QFE so you need to take into account the height of the ground when calculating your safe transit altitude. It is also good practice for pilots intending to transit the vicinity of an aerodrome to call ahead in sufficient time to request relevant aerodrome and traffic information and to alert other pilots and ATC about the transit.

NOTES:

NEAR MISS

CHIRP

Feb 2014, Issue 59

The weather was overcast 8/8ths, cloud base about 2000 ft AMSL. I was at 1500 ft on the QNH and speaking to a LARS unit before switching to ZZZ Radio. On requesting airfield information for a touch and-go, I was advised the runway in use and circuit direction, given the QFE and was advised "no traffic to affect". I had just dialled up the QFE and was about to commence a right turn to join downwind [from a position 2 miles due east of the aerodrome] when my passenger pointed out an aircraft at the same height. It was in my 2 o'clock on a reciprocal course, so it was between me the airfield. I would estimate the separation as we passed to be between 200 and 300 metres. The other aircraft continued on a northerly course. I took no avoiding action because, (1) although it was quite close, the other aircraft was not on a collision course and (2) he was abeam and past before I could react. I asked the air/ground operator if he had any other aircraft on frequency and he confirmed he had not. On landing I sought the views of radio operators and instructors. The general opinion was that the aircraft I saw should have spoken to ZZZ Radio before approaching as close as he did (no more than 2 NM).

Lessons Learned:

1. When an air/ground radio operator says "no traffic to affect" it doesn't mean there isn't any. It means there is none that he is aware of.
2. When the cloud base is 2000 ft everyone is going to be flying between 1500 and 1900 ft - i.e. virtually the same height.

Suggestions: Keep a good lookout even when you think there's nothing out there and always speak to an airfield you are about to overfly or approach within 2 or 3 miles.

CHIRP Comment: Since this occurrence was not reported as an AirProx it is not possible to know whether the other pilot was in visual contact with the reporter's aircraft. However, it is poor airmanship and a frequent cause of AirProx incidents that pilots fly too close to aerodromes without announcing their presence on the RT. Since A/G operators are unlikely to be aware of transiting traffic that has not called on the RT, they are required to use the phraseology that there is "no reported traffic". Whatever is said on the RT, in Class G airspace pilots should maintain a vigilant look out at all times and, as in this case, 'expect the unexpected'.

NOTES:

CLOSE ENCOUNTER

CHIRP

Nov 2013, Issue 58

Returning to my local airstrip on a clear fine day I made several blind calls stating my intentions that included turning base and turning finals. As I turned base leg keeping as I thought a good lookout, I raised the nose of my aircraft and set the flaps for landing; this gave me a nose high attitude and obscured an approaching motor glider that I had failed to spot earlier, low against the hills and trees. Although my aircraft has good forward visibility, the approaching aircraft was now in my blind spot on a converging course. I called and turned "finals" keeping a good lookout at the runway and clearing my turn; all this time the converging aircraft remained in my blind spot being obscured by the nose of my aircraft and was closing on a constant bearing as I turned.

As I completed my turn levelling the wings I spotted the converging aircraft very close and at the same height. A swift turn to my right resolved the conflict and I continued with my landing.

I later found and chatted to the other pilot. Neither the other experienced pilot nor his also experienced passenger saw my aircraft at any time during the incident; they both considered that they were keeping a good lookout particularly as they were passing the airfield at low level (500 ft) close in and intersecting the finals glide path. The other pilot was not monitoring the airfield frequency and did not hear my calls. He concluded that he had chosen the worst possible place to pass the airfield and at the worst possible height; he was also mortified that he hadn't seen me even during my steep close turn.

In conclusion, his aircraft was on my right and had right of way. He was returning to his airfield some three miles away and chose the worst place and height to be. We both did not keep an adequate lookout. He acknowledges that he should have been monitoring the airfield frequency. He subsequently briefed other pilots at his airfield on the incident, circuits and frequency etc. I concluded that I need to look for the unexpected, particularly low in the background clutter and to keep a better lookout.

CHIRP Comment: Flying through the overhead of a neighbouring airstrip at 500 ft without making any R/T transmissions was poor airmanship. If you know the location of an airfield or airstrip either stay well clear of the traffic pattern or make a radio call on the airfield frequency and plan your transit to avoid any aircraft already established in the traffic pattern.

NOTES:

CHAPTER 8

TECHNOLOGY & AUTOMATION

"I was always afraid of dying. Always. It was my fear that made me learn everything I could about my airplane and my emergency equipment, and kept me flying respectful of my machine and always alert in the cockpit."

General Chuck Yeager

IPAD AND COMPASS DEVIATION

CHIRP

Feb 2016, Issue 67

We were on a land away NAVEX. The student's NAV plan was working out well. Having obtained clearance to transit CTA, we were asked not to come any further east as xxx had a departure. To confirm my position with respect to xxx, I picked up the iPad mini from the back seat, checked our position and then placed it on the aircraft coaming. I then checked the compass and assumed that the student had drifted 25 degrees off the required heading.

He then re-synchronised the DI and we continued on the wrong heading. After a short while ATC queried our routing, and provided a suggested heading towards our chosen VRP. I realised what had happened. I had placed the iPad close to the compass, and had introduced a huge deviation. I removed the tablet to the back seat, and the compass returned to normal. We returned to xxx without further problem following the student's NAV plan.

Lessons Learned:

1. We know about treating GPS with respect due to satellite problems, and possible incorrect programming. But I hadn't considered the physical problem of the steel case. It will stay on the back seat unless I am using it.
2. Accept the compass could be indicating incorrectly, and the need to carry out the "lost procedure" earlier.
3. Be wary of placing any metal or electric object near the compass.

CHIRP Comment: We agree with the lessons learned. Any object containing or constructed from ferrous metal or magnetic material and any phone, tablet or other electronic device has the potential to affect magnetic instruments and should be kept as far away as possible. A couple of other things: tablets left on coamings can fail due to overheating and/or, as they are thin, it is possible for them to be out of sight and forgotten on a high coaming that slopes down towards the windscreen.

NOTES:

DEGRADED RNAV

CALLBACK

Feb, 2017, Issue 445

On my first approach attempt, the reported weather indicated a 300 foot ceiling with 2.5 miles visibility. I was established on the RNAV (GPS) RWY 31 approach, and shortly after the FAF, the approach downgraded to LNAV. The weather was below [LNAV] minimums, so I declared a missed approach and requested the RNAV (GPS) RWY 31 approach into [a nearby airport]. After the IAF, approximately at the FAF, the approach downgraded to an LNAV approach. I was high on final and declared a missed approach. By this time, I was lower on fuel than I expected and advised ATC of the situation. ATC advised that they would provide the ILS RWY 13 approach to save time. The receiver did not provide accurate glide slope, but ATC advised altitudes at the fixes and a landing was made without incident. I intend to practice more ILS approaches and also LNAV approaches.

NOTES:

GPS GUIDES TO DISTRACTION

CASA

by David Julian, Nov 18, 2014

As I completed my daily inspection, I reflected on the flying I'd done in the past couple of weeks. We'd been following 'Air Shows In The Outback' around western Queensland and offering joy flights to the spectators. With a fascinating array of aircraft—warbirds, vintage, ultralights, aerobatic, and even balloons—the shows had attracted big crowds. Demand had far exceeded our expectations and it had been a lot of fun, but open cockpit flying is tiring at the best of times so I was glad to finally be heading home.

The ground crew had a long way to drive so they'd left early and as I taxied the Tiger Moth out I realised that without assistance the wind was going to make backtracking on the sealed runway a handful —given the tail-skid and lack of brakes. I didn't need a lot of runway and beyond the boundary fence was a nice clear paddock, so there was somewhere to go if the engine failed on take-off. I decided on an intersection departure and proceeded down the taxiway to the holding point. I made sure my map board was firmly strapped to my leg and turned on the GPS that was velcroed on top of it.

Completing the pre-take-off checks by ensuring the controls had full travel.

I pulled my goggles down, turned onto the runway and lined up. I opened the throttle, the Gipsy Major engine responded with a roar and as the plane accelerated I pushed the stick forward and the tail came up. A quick check of RPM and oil pressure showed everything normal, and I eased the stick back. She seemed reluctant to unstick initially, so I applied a little more back pressure and checked the airspeed, which was climbing through 40 knots.

By now we should have been airborne but something didn't feel right. I pulled back a bit harder, and then the realisation hit me, the stick was jammed!

I immediately closed the throttle, but by now the end of the runway was approaching fast so I switched off the magnetos and, as the propeller slowed to a stop, I resisted an urge to push on absent brake pedals.

I couldn't get the tail down to use the drag of the skid and the speed wasn't washing off fast enough. The tail finally came down as we rolled off the runway into the dirt, and with the fence rapidly looming closer I kicked full right rudder and we slid sideways to a stop in a cloud of dust a couple of metres from the fence.

I sat in the cockpit, shaking, with the heightened awareness that comes with a good dose of adrenaline. The quiet and calm seemed surreal after those few seconds of panic and as I slowly lifted my goggles I could smell the settling red dust and hot engine oil. I was lucky—very lucky—to get away without a scratch on the aeroplane, or myself. But what had gone wrong?

I tried the stick again, lateral movement was fine and I could push it forward, but it wouldn't move back at all. I climbed out of the cockpit, took my jacket off and then undid the strap on the map board and put it on the seat. As I did so, I noticed the GPS was missing and quickly looked on the cockpit floor with no sign of it. Then I saw it, jammed between the joystick and the back of the control box. When

I pulled it out, the face had a groove in it where the base of the stick had been pushing on it.

With the map board on my left knee, my jacket sleeve must have caught on the GPS. As I opened the throttle the movement had dislodged it, allowing it to drop down the front of the seat and into the gap behind the stick, just as I pushed the stick forward to lift the tail.

Ten minutes later as I taxied slowly to the far end of the runway, I reflected on how, once again, a series of things had 'lined up' to cause an emergency.

My jacket sleeve catching the GPS as I opened the throttle, the fact that it fell in the right orientation, in the right place, just as I pushed the stick forward.

It was exactly the right size to lodge there and block the stick, and my decision to use an intersection departure left insufficient runway at the critical moment. A valuable lesson learned at the cost of only a few white hairs!

NOTES:

TOO SMUG FOR COMFORT
CASA

Name withheld by request, Jul 15, 2014

Another very experienced pilot and I were flying a Conquest back to home base after dropping off a load of passengers. We knew the aircraft, route and airspace like the backs of our hands, we both had a couple of thousand hours in the Conquest, and normally flew single-pilot IFR, so two-crew operations were a perfect opportunity for a good chin wag (and, in hindsight, for some serious mistakes).

We did everything without really thinking about it and completed the checks in record time.

As we turned onto heading and climbed through 4000 feet I noticed that the runway rising indicator and the glide slope indicator were stuck together inside the artificial horizon. The aircraft was flying as per normal and it was a gin-clear day all the way home so I did not see it as a major problem. Having never seen this bizarre malfunction before I casually remarked how odd it was. As we continued home, we started trouble-shooting the system; pulling circuit breakers, changing modes, testing the radar altimeter function, all in an attempt to correct the minor inconvenience.

Route clearance was given and I stopped playing with the knobs and switches for long enough to read back the clearance and dial it into the GPS—but then I noticed something else out of the ordinary. I didn't have the correct way point in the GPS ...

I immediately realised my mistake; I had simply reversed the route (a one-way route) in the GPS and was cleared back home via another one-way route that kept inbound and outbound aircraft separated as they funnelled into our capital city. 'What an idiot! Ah well, no problem.' In six seconds flat I was able to dial up the route required, check it over and get us heading in the right direction. Problem solved, back to chatting about how we could fix our annoying indication issue. Sadly, my complacency had made me miss a major red flag.

We settled into the cruise at FL250 and, having exhausted our options for the artificial horizon anomaly, left it at that and started busily planning lunch, his retirement and my upcoming job interview.

Along the way we were told to lose more than six minutes for our arrival point (a major blow to our lunch plans) and we pleaded with the controller to try and slot us into another runway or squeeze us into the pattern a little earlier. At 350 knots we were keen to keep that ground speed up, but the controller was not having a bar of it and asked us if we would like vectors—the internationally recognised way for controllers to signal the impending end of a conversation.

Disappointed, I declined and pulled the power levers to flight idle.

We resumed our conversation and watched as the ground speed peeled back from an enjoyable 350 knots into the depressingly low 200s.

As we approached our arrival point a red annunciation CABIN ALTITUDE lit up on the warning panel. Neither of us had experienced this before but it meant that the cabin altitude was above 11,500 feet. At 35,000 feet the Conquest can hold 10,900 feet cabin altitude, so this was a definite surprise, considering we were 10,000 feet below that.

We stopped discussing trivialities and started trouble shooting. He pulled the circuit breaker that allows the passenger oxygen masks to deploy (even though they are one hell of a thing to replace in the roof lining) and increased the cabin heating (this helps to increase cabin descent), while I set the cabin in a descent, powered up the engines to provide more bleed air and started our descent a little early to help the entire process out.

Once we got the cabin descending the light went out and we continued home, using the SOPs in a more professional manner.

The cabin had been in a slow descent from the moment I pulled back the power (a cold cabin and very low power setting means the pressurisation system struggles to maintain altitude). If we had been paying attention one of us would have scanned the cabin altitude and noticed the issue earlier.

If we had been paying attention …

Two very experienced pilots flying an aircraft that can easily be flown by just one, on a perfectly clear day, in familiar airspace, had managed through simple inattention to get behind the aircraft. As says the law of sod; right when you think everything is fine is when it will decide to bite.

Aircraft will do that if you don't keep an eye on them and yourself.

Stay steely and watch out for red flags whatever and whenever you are flying.

NOTES:

GONE PEAR SHAPED

CASA

Name withheld by request, Mar 28, 2014

Think you'll never be seduced into relying on GPS instead of airmanship? Think again.

How much do we rely on GPS? More and more, until we are now almost entirely dependent upon its accuracy and continued operation. But it wasn't always that way—we used to teach proper navigation skills (dead reckoning, 1 in 60 rule etc.) Once, we used to draw tracks on paper charts and mark our times and estimates with a strange-looking thing called a pencil.

I encountered an early adopter of the then-new technology while I was instructing in New Zealand in 1995. While flying a routine IFR NAVEX with a student, I overheard the RNZAF Ohakea controller calling an unknown aircraft that had ventured into his airspace from the north without the requisite clearance. After some minutes, the pilot responded and after a few turns for identification, was asked exactly what his intentions were.

It turned out that he was lost and above cloud, after having departed an airfield somewhere north of Auckland earlier that morning, using his new GPS for navigation. His wife had bought the unit for him and encouraged him to go and use it, so that is exactly what he had set out to do. The only problem was that he hadn't taken the instruction book with him to assist with his learning. Nor had he taken any paper charts for backup. Also, he hadn't been keeping an accurate log, so he now found himself in military airspace, above cloud, and with an increasingly frustrated controller intent on getting him out of there. He was vectored to land at Ohakea, where he was presumably dealt with in a more formal manner. I never saw the incident mentioned in any safety magazine or other media, but I can only assume that he was eventually released and allowed to resume his trip, hopefully with some paper charts to assist.

Another incident occurred in the United States, when I was flying with a student on a two-hour, commercial NAVEX. Let's call her Lauren for this story. The night before, I had asked Lauren to prepare her chart and nav log for the trip, and to make any notes she felt she needed in order to be comfortable and prepared. I had also asked her to draw 10-mile hacks on each leg. However, this seems not to be something that the American system is too familiar with, as Lauren had never heard of them and I had to briefly explain their intended use. In spite of all this, she arrived for the flight with not a mark on her chart—not even her tracks! I decided to leave the subject alone for the moment and allow her to continue with her preparations.

I had flown some instrument training exercises with her, but as this was her first VFR NAVEX with me, I thought I'd just let her do her own thing for a while and I could debrief her later and/or fix any problems as they cropped up.

Life was about to get very complicated for Lauren though, as immediately after departure I simulated a low cloud base and would not allow her above 500 feet AGL. I wasn't intending to cause her any real problems, but Lauren's actions at this time quickly set the scene for a great learning experience for both of us. Before we had even reached 500 feet, Lauren was manoeuvring to track via the VFR

GPS fitted to the control column of the little Grumman Tiger. I reached over and turned it off, reminding her that this was to be a visual NAVEX and she would have to find an alternative method to fix her position. She immediately dialled up the nearest VOR and attempted to navigate with that. Of course, at 500 feet, there was little accuracy in the signal anyway, but I also turned that off, attempting to make a point that she seemed determined to miss. Americans don't like to use NDBs very much, but just in case, I also turned that off before Lauren even thought to dial it up.

After a couple of minutes, it was clear to me that Lauren had neither logged her departure time, nor calculated the ETA for her first turning point, and every additional minute saw us travelling further off track as she already had a 15-degree error in her heading. Consequently, she was lost within minutes of departure—and we would still have been within sight of our departure airport if we had turned around. It was clearly time to revisit 'Map reading 101' and very quickly, as I didn't want to turn around and scrub the sortie because we had to pick up another aircraft at our destination.

I took control of the aircraft and asked Lauren to draw lines and 10-mile hacks on her chart, after which I proceeded to re-teach her how to navigate visually, using first the larger landmarks, and then progressively smaller features to confirm and fine tune her plotting. Given that she already had over 200 hours of experience, I had expected a much better start to our trip, but it was not going to be a waste of time if I could help it.

Over the next 45 minutes or so, I continued to fly the aircraft and instruct quite heavily, with little opportunity for Lauren to do anything but listen and do as I asked. After that, I let her have the aircraft again while she applied her new-found skills and knowledge to get us to the second waypoint. By the time we got to our destination a little over an hour later, she was becoming comfortable with the technique and not even missing the GPS.

More recently, I left Coober Pedy, using the GPS as primary navigation source on an IFR flight, but as I adjusted the settings the unit's screen went blank. I now had to navigate using only the NDB, and that was quickly falling further behind me. There were no NAVAIDS in front of me on this track, but fortunately, it was a clear day and I could easily see where I was going. After a quick reboot, the unit told me we were somewhere in Europe—clearly not quite right, but at least showing it was ready to TRY and find our position. I also had an iPad with a basic navigation application, from which I was able to obtain a latitude and longitude to input into my sadly 'dumb' GPS unit. Finally, I had both position and track back on the GPS display, and continued to my destination without further difficulty. However, as a precaution, I remained VMC and kept a very good log of my progress in order to double check that we stayed on track.

It was one of those 'there I was' stories for the bar or BBQ, but had the conditions been IMC, it would have been an entirely different proposition. I too had fallen into the trap of relying too much on just one system! With the stunning accuracy of GPS and the ease with which we can get around on our typically low-stress flights, it is very easy for complacency to creep in, and suddenly, to find ourselves without that essential bit of information to keep our passengers and ourselves safe—just where the hell we are.

NOTES:

CHAPTER 9

ON THE GROUND

**"There are two critical points in every aerial flight —
its beginning and its end."**
Alexander Graham Bell
1906

VEHICLE ON THE RUNWAY

GROUND MOVEMENTS AWARENESS CHIRP

Nov 2016, Issue 70

The airfield has a grass runway on private land (a farm estate) with a centre portion paved/concrete. It is home to a number of non-aviation clubs. This runway section is crossed by users of the airfield in vehicles in order to reach the hangars. A prominent warning sign warns drivers to look to both sides for aircraft.

I was landing and was aware of a 4x4 vehicle moving on the airfield. Within 3 to 5 seconds of this initial sighting I was touching down on the NE runway when the vehicle without stopping drove (from the left) onto the runway paved area and started an unhurried U turn in a clockwise direction. The only course of action I had was to use heavier than usual braking - however the aircraft was not going to slow down like a car might with emergency braking on the cut grass. I steered to the left whilst the vehicle driver completed the U turn and noticed me in time to accelerate off the paved area. Had he not accelerated off we would either have collided or at best I'd have had to aim off runway. Attempting a go around once I had touched down was out of the question.

The driver high tailed it down the roadway to leave the farm property - I had turned the aircraft around hoping to make a note of the Registration number though this was not possible. I asked around but no-one was able to identify the vehicle or its driver. The driver clearly realised the seriousness of his careless action and rather than stop and apologise has demonstrated a reckless disregard for safety. Never have I been so in fear of my life.

The [ ] VFR Flight Guide does contain a warning for visiting pilots that uncontrolled movements of vehicles near the runway are to be watched out for.

Lessons Learned:

I have flown from this airfield for just over 20 years, so well acquainted with activities typical of many farms needing to diversify. Awareness during take-off is perhaps more obvious, and likewise when in the circuit planning to land. However during the final phase of a landing, when flaring, one's attention is very much on the task in hand. Never before had I considered a drill for such an eventuality - and is probably one that needs to be shared with new members operating at our airfield.

CHIRP Comment: The reporter has highlighted the need for extraordinary vigilance to guard against traffic/people/animals on unlicensed runways at mixed use airfields. It is essential that all users of such airfields and airfield operators meet regularly to review and agree appropriate procedures, signage and barriers to minimise the hazards. As a runway incursion, this incident involving an EASA certificated aircraft (e.g. Cessna, Piper etc) is a reportable event (by Mandatory Occurrence Report) for licensed and unlicensed airfields. (Had the reporter been flying an Annex II aircraft the incident would have warranted a voluntary report).

NOTES:

AVGAS CONTAMINATION

GROUND MOVEMENTS AWARENESS CHIRP

Aug 2016, Issue 69

I am the owner of a Cessna 172 which is hangared in [ ]. I was recently up at the hangar checking on my plane when the local farmer came in; he informed me not to use my Avgas as it has been contaminated.

How? At some point in February the JetA1 bowser on the airfield was having its service and filters changed by an external service company, with all the excess fuel which had accumulated during the filter change the service person thought it would be convenient to dispose of the JetA1 in the nearest drum he could find, this turned out to be my half full drum of Avgas which I was planning on using this week.

The drum is a designated [proprietary] Avgas drum, blue and clearly labelled and sitting not too far from a piston engine aeroplane.

Thanks to the farmer informing me of this otherwise it would have gone into my tanks.

CHIRP Comment: Well done that farmer! This was a serious incident with the potential to turn out very badly indeed. It demonstrates that clearly labelling a container does not guarantee that the label will be read. The answer seems to be locking fuel drums securely so that they cannot be accessed by irresponsible or incompetent third parties. Also, if aircraft have lockable fuel tanks, remember to use them as fuel theft is not unknown.

NOTES:

AIR GROUND COMMUNICATIONS
GROUND MOVEMENTS AWARENESS CHIRP

Aug 2016, Issue 69

I was carrying out a flight to [ ]. Despite flying the planned route many times previously, I read numerous sections of the AIP, including the entry for [ ] to make sure I was up to date with procedures.

I free called [ ] Radio requesting joining information. I received the airfield details which I read back and joined overhead as per published procedure. On landing I was holding the nose of the aircraft off the runway and slowing down without brakes when the AGCS told me to, "vacate at Bravo". Once I had slowed the aircraft I vacated at B and was instructed by the AGCS operator to, "Taxi to the end of Bravo and park on the concrete as the grass is soft". I was fully aware that an AGCS cannot give instructions, however I complied with them as they know the surface conditions better than I do and understood they were only trying to help.

On departure I again called [ ] Radio asking for taxi information for a flight to [ ]. I was given the airfield details and also a taxi instruction to, "Taxi to holding point Alpha". Again, I know that

AGCS cannot give taxi instructions and due to my pre-flight planning I had already decided that I was going to taxi to Alpha anyway.

To somebody who has an understanding of the different types of Air Traffic Service Unit (ATSU) it wasn't such a big problem; however, I see more and more students as well as PPLs who are confused by the three types of ATSU and actions like the one described above only further blur the important distinctions between the services. I recently witnessed a runway incursion where a pilot simply taxied onto an active runway in front of a solo student at an AFIS unit without calling because he thought AFIS didn't control him on the ground. Ignoring the pilot's disregard for the basic rules of the air, his understanding that he could line up at an AFIS unit without approval stemmed from his misunderstanding of the services which is only exaggerated when airfields don't stick to the rules. The solo student had to go-around from low level to avoid a collision. What makes matters worse is I train students in correct RT procedures and the limits of the services and when they fly to other airfields expecting one thing and receive something totally different it doesn't just confuse them - it also makes my teaching look incorrect.

Lessons Learned:

As AGCS operators only have to pass a Radio Operator's Certificate of Competence (ROCC), are not technically licensed and are not as closely regulated as Flight Information Service Officers and Air Traffic Control Officers. I believe a simple letter or information poster being sent to holders of a ROCC may help to reduce the amount of incorrect phraseology and services being provided.

CHIRP Comment: The AGCS operator was undoubtedly trying to be as helpful as possible but the reporter is correct in highlighting the risks of allowing the Air/Ground service to stray from information to instructions. Despite the use of the call sign "xxx Radio", which identifies the service as an Air/Ground service, inexperienced pilots are particularly at risk of treating AGCS instructions as authoritative.

NOTES:

CHAPTER 10

FURTHER READING

IF YOU ENJOYED READING *81 Lessons From The Sky*, then you might also enjoy the other books in the *Lessons From The Sky* series.

51 Lessons From The Sky (US Air Force)
61 Lessons From The Sky (Military Helicopters)
71 Lessons From The Sky (Civilian Helicopters)
101 Lessons From The Sky (Commercial Aviation)
Top Gun Lessons From The Sky (US Navy)

Do you have any lessons you would like to share with Fletcher, and the aviation community? Email them to Fletcher at **fletch@avgasgroup.com** for him to share on his social media accounts, or to include in a future book. Please note that if you do send through any lessons, you are giving us permission to publish those stories.

GLOSSARY

A

A Amber

AAA (or AAB, AAC . . . etc., in sequence) Amended meteorological
message (message type designator)

A/A Air-to-air

AAD Assigned altitude deviation

AAIM Aircraft autonomous integrity monitoring

AAL Above aerodrome level

ABI Advance boundary information

ABM Abeam

ABN Aerodrome beacon

ABT About

ABV Above

AC Altocumulus

ACAM Airborne collision avoidance system

ACARS† Aircraft communication addressing and reporting system

ACAS† Airborne collision avoidance system

ACC‡ Area control centre or area control

ACCID Notification of an aircraft accident

ACFT Aircraft

ACK Acknowledge

ACL Altimeter check location

ACN Aircraft classification number

ACP Acceptance (message type designator)

ACPT Accept or accepted

ACT Active or activated or activity

AD Aerodrome

ADA Advisory area

ADC Aerodrome chart

ADDN Addition or additional

ADF‡ Automatic direction-finding equipment

ADIZ† Air defence identification zone

ADJ Adjacent

ADO Aerodrome office (specify service)

ADR Advisory route

ADS* The address (when this abbreviation is used to request a repetition, the question mark (IMI) precedes the abbreviation, e.g. IMI ADS) (to be used in AFS as a procedure signal)

AGL Above ground level

ALERFA† Alert phase

ALR Alerting (message type designator)

ALRS Alerting service

ALS Approach lighting system

ALT Altitude

ALTN Alternate or alternating (light alternates in colour)

ALTN Alternate (aerodrome)

AMA Area minimum altitude

AMD Amend or amended (used to indicate amended meteorological message; message type designator)

AMDT Amendment (AIP Amendment)

AMS Aeronautical mobile service

AMSL Above mean sea level

AMSS Aeronautical mobile satellite service

ANC . . . Aeronautical chart — 1:500 000 (followed by name/title)

ANCS . . . Aeronautical navigation chart — small scale (followed by name/title and scale)

ANS Answer

AOC . . . Aerodrome obstacle chart (followed by type and name/title)

AP Airport

APAPI† Abbreviated precision approach path indicator

APCH Approach

APDC . . . Aircraft parking/docking chart (followed by name/title)

APN Apron

APP Approach control office or approach control or approach control service

APR April

APRX Approximate or approximately

APSG After passing

APV Approve or approved or approval

ARC Area chart

ARNG Arrange

ARO Air traffic services reporting office

ARP Aerodrome reference point

ARP Air-report (message type designator)

ARQ Automatic error correction

ARR Arrival (message type designator)

ARR Arrive or arrival

ARS Special air-report (message type designator)

ARST Arresting (specify (part of) aircraft arresting equipment)

AS Altostratus

ASC Ascend to or ascending to

ASDA Accelerate-stop distance available

ASE Altimetry system error

ASHTAM Special series NOTAM notifying, by means of a specific format, change in activity of a volcano, a volcanic eruption and/or volcanic ash cloud that is of significance to aircraft operations

ASPH Asphalt

AT ... At (followed by time at which weather change is forecast to occur)

ATA‡ Actual time of arrival

ATC‡ Air traffic control (in general)

ATCSMAC... Air traffic control surveillance minimum altitude chart (followed by name/title)

ATD‡ Actual time of departure

ATFM Air traffic flow management

ATIS† Automatic terminal information service

ATM Air traffic management

ATN Aeronautical telecommunication network

ATP ... At ... (time or place)

ATS Air traffic services

ATTN Attention

AT-VASIS† Abbreviated T visual approach slope indicator system

ATZ Aerodrome traffic zone

AUG August

AUTH Authorised or authorisation

AUW All up weight

AUX Auxiliary

AVBL Available or availability

AVG Average

AVGAS† Aviation gasoline

AWTA Advise at what time able

AWY Airway

AZM Azimuth

B

B Blue

BA Braking action

BARO-VNAV† Barometric vertical navigation

BASE† Cloud base

BCFG Fog patches
BCN Beacon (aeronautical ground light)
BCST Broadcast
BDRY Boundary
BECMG Becoming
BFR Before
BKN Broken
BL . . . Blowing (followed by DU = dust, SA = sand or SN = snow)
BLDG Building
BLO Below clouds
BLW . . . Below . . .
BOMB Bombing
BR Mist
BRF Short (used to indicate the type of approach desired or required)
BRG Bearing
BRKG Braking
BS Commercial broadcasting station
BTL Between layers
BTN Between
BUFR Binary universal form for the representation of meteorological
data

C

. . . C Centre (preceded by runway designation number to identify a
parallel runway)
C Degrees Celsius (Centigrade)
CA Course to an altitude
CAT Category
CAT Clear air turbulence
CAVOK† Visibility, cloud and present weather better than
prescribed values or conditions
CB‡ Cumulonimbus
CC Cirrocumulus

CCA (or CCB, CCC . . . etc., in sequence) Corrected meteorological message (message type designator)

CD Candela

CDN Coordination (message type designator)

CF Change frequency to . . .

CF Course to a fix

CFM* Confirm or I confirm (to be used in AFS as a procedure signal)

CGL Circling guidance light(s)

CH Channel

CH# This is a channel-continuity-check of transmission to permit comparison of your record of channel sequence numbers of messages received on the channel (to be used in AFS as a procedure signal)

CHEM Chemical

CHG Modification (message type designator)

CI Cirrus

CIDIN† Common ICAO data interchange network

CIT Near or over large towns

CIV Civil

CK Check

CL Centre line

CLA Clear type of ice formation

CLBR Calibration

CLD Cloud

CLG Calling

CLIMB-OUT Climb-out area

CLR Clear(s) or cleared to . . . or clearance

CLRD Runway(s) cleared (used in METAR/SPECI)

CLSD Close or closed or closing

CM Centimetre

CMB Climb to or climbing to

CMPL Completion or completed or complete

CNL Cancel or cancelled

CNL Flight plan cancellation (message type designator)

CNS Communications, navigation and surveillance

COM Communications
CONC Concrete
COND Condition
CONS Continuous
CONST Construction or constructed
CONT Continue(s) or continued
COOR Coordinate or coordination
COORD Coordinates
COP Change-over point
COR Correct or correction or corrected (used to indicate corrected meteorological message; message type designator)
COT At the coast
COV Cover or covered or covering
CPDLC‡ Controller-pilot data link communications
CPL Current flight plan (message type designator)
CRC Cyclic redundancy check
CRM Collision risk model
CRZ Cruise
CS Call sign
CS Cirrostratus
CTA Control area
CTAM Climb to and maintain
CTC Contact
CTL Control
CTN Caution
CTR Control zone
CU Cumulus
CUF Cumuliform
CUST Customs
CVR Cockpit voice recorder
CW Continuous wave
CWY Clearway

D

D Downward (tendency in RVR during previous 10 minutes)
D . . . Danger area (followed by identification)
DA Decision altitude
D-ATIS† Data link automatic terminal information service
DCD Double channel duplex
DCKG Docking
DCP Datum crossing point
DCPC Direct controller-pilot communications
DCS Double channel simplex
DCT Direct (in relation to flight plan clearances and type of approach)
DE* From (used to precede the call sign of the calling station) (to be used in AFS as a procedure signal)
DEC December
DEG Degrees
DEP Depart or departure
DEP Departure (message type designator)
DEPO Deposition
DER Departure end of the runway
DES Descend to or descending to
DEST Destination
DETRESFA† Distress phase
DEV Deviation or deviating
DF Direction finding
DFDR Digital flight data recorder
DFTI Distance from touchdown indicator
DH Decision height
DIF Diffuse
DIST Distance
DIV Divert or diverting
DLA Delay or delayed
DLA Delay (message type designator)
DLIC Data link initiation capability
DLY Daily

DME‡ Distance measuring equipment

DNG Danger or dangerous

DOM Domestic

DP Dew point temperature

DPT Depth

DR Dead reckoning

DR . . . Low drifting (followed by DU = dust, SA = sand or SN = snow)

DRG During

DS Dust-storm

DSB Double sideband

DTAM Descend to and maintain

DTG Date-time group

DTHR Displaced runway threshold

DTRT Deteriorate or deteriorating

DTW Dual tandem wheels

DU Dust

DUC Dense upper cloud

DUPE# This is a duplicate message (to be used in AFS as a procedure signal)

DUR Duration

D-VOLMET Data link VOLMET

DVOR Doppler VOR

DW Dual wheels

DZ Drizzle

E

E East or eastern longitude

EATExpected approach time

EB Eastbound

EDA Elevation differential area

EEE# Error (to be used in AFS as a procedure signal)

EET Estimated elapsed time

EFC Expect further clearance

EFIS† Electronic flight instrument system

EGNOS† European geostationary navigation overlay service

EHF Extremely high frequency [30 000 to 300 000 MHz]

ELBA† Emergency location beacon — aircraft

ELEV Elevation

ELR Extra long range

ELT Emergency locator transmitter

EM Emission

EMBD Embedded in a layer (to indicate cumulonimbus embedded in layers of other clouds)

EMERG Emergency

END Stop-end (related to RVR)

ENE East-north-east

ENG Engine

ENR En route

ENRC . . . En route chart (followed by name/title)

EOBT Estimated off-block time

EQPT Equipment

ER* Here . . . or herewith

ESE East-south-east

EST Estimate or estimated or estimation (message type designator)

ETA*‡ Estimated time of arrival or estimating arrival

ETD‡ Estimated time of departure or estimating departure

ETO Estimated time over significant point

EUR RODEX European regional OPMET data exchange

EV Every

EVS Enhanced vision system

EXC Except

EXER Exercises or exercising or to exercise

EXP Expect or expected or expecting

EXTD Extend or extending

F

F Fixed

FA Course from a fix to an altitude

FAC Facilities

FAF Final approach fix

FAL Facilitation of international air transport

FAP Final approach point

FAS Final approach segment

FATO Final approach and take-off area

FAX Facsimile transmission

FBL Light (used to indicate the intensity of weather phenomena, interference or static reports, e.g. FBL RA = light rain)

FC Funnel cloud (tornado or water spout)

FCST Forecast

FCT Friction coefficient

FDPS Flight data processing system

FEB February

FEW Few

FG Fog

FIC Flight information centre

FIR‡ Flight information region

FIS Flight information service

FISA Automated flight information service

FISO (non ICAO) - Flight Information Service Officers (UK)

FL Flight level

FLD Field

FLG Flashing

FLR Flares

FLT Flight

FLTCK Flight check

FLUC Fluctuating or fluctuation or fluctuated

FLW Follow(s) or following

FLY Fly or flying

FM Course from a fix to manual termination (used in navigation database coding)

FM From

FM . . . From (followed by time weather change is forecast to begin)

FMC Flight management computer

FMS‡ Flight management system

FMU Flow management unit

FNA Final approach

FPAP Flight path alignment point

FPL Filed flight plan (message type designator)

FPM Feet per minute

FPR Flight plan route

FR Fuel remaining

FREQ Frequency

FRI Friday

FRNG Firing

FRONT† Front (relating to weather)

FROST† Frost (used in aerodrome warnings)

FRQ Frequent

FSL Full stop landing

FSS Flight service station

FST First

FT Feet (dimensional unit)

FTE Flight technical error

FTP Fictitious threshold point

FTT Flight technical tolerance

FU Smoke

FZ Freezing

FZDZ Freezing drizzle

FZFG Freezing fog

FZRA Freezing rain

G

G Green

G ... Variations from the mean wind speed (gusts) (followed by figures in METAR/SPECI and TAF)

GA Go ahead, resume sending (to be used in AFS as a procedure signal)

G/A Ground-to-air

G/A/G Ground-to-air and air-to-ground

GAGAN† GPS and geostationary earth orbit augmented navigation

GAIN Airspeed or headwind gain

GAMET Area forecast for low-level flights

GARP GBAS azimuth reference point

GBAS† Ground-based augmentation system

GCA‡ Ground controlled approach system or ground controlled approach

GEN General

GEO Geographic or true

GES Ground earth station

GLD Glider

GLONASS† Global orbiting navigation satellite system

GLS‡ GBAS landing system

GMC ... Ground movement chart (followed by name/title)

GND Ground

GNDCK Ground check

GNSS‡ Global navigation satellite system

GP Glide path

GPA Glide path angle

GPIP Glide path intercept point

GPS‡ Global positioning system

GPWS‡ Ground proximity warning system

GR Hail

GRAS† Ground-based regional augmentation system

GRASS Grass landing area

GRIB Processed meteorological data in the form of grid point values expressed in binary form (meteorological code)

GRVL Gravel

GS Ground speed
GS Small hail and/or snow pellets
GUND Geoid undulation

H

H High pressure area or the centre of high pressure
H24 Continuous day and night service
HA Holding/racetrack to an altitude
HAPI Helicopter approach path indicator
HBN Hazard beacon
HDF High frequency direction-finding station
HDG Heading
HEL Helicopter
HF‡ High frequency [3 000 to 30 000 kHz]
HF Holding/racetrack to a fix
HGT Height or height above
HJ Sunrise to sunset
HLDG Holding
HM Holding/racetrack to a manual termination
HN Sunset to sunrise
HO Service available to meet operational requirements
HOL Holiday
HOSP Hospital aircraft
HPA Hectopascal
HR Hours
HS Service available during hours of scheduled operations
HUD Head-up display
HURCN Hurricane
HVDF High and very high frequency direction finding stations (at the same location)
HVY Heavy
HVY Heavy (used to indicate the intensity of weather phenomena, e.g. HVY RA = heavy rain)

HX No specific working hours
HYR Higher
HZ Haze
HZ Hertz (cycle per second)

I

IAC . . . Instrument approach chart (followed by name/title)
IAF Initial approach fix
IAO In and out of clouds
IAP Instrument approach procedure
IARIntersection of air routes
IAS Indicated airspeed
IBN Identification beacon
IC Ice crystals (very small ice crystals in suspension, also known as diamond dust)
ICE Icing
ID Identifier or identify
IDENT† Identification
IF Intermediate approach fix
IFF Identification friend/foe
IFR‡ Instrument flight rules
IGA International general aviation
ILS‡ Instrument landing system
IM Inner marker
IMC‡ Instrument meteorological conditions
IMG Immigration
IMI* Interrogation sign (question mark) (to be used in AFS as a procedure signal)
IMPR Improve or improving
IMT Immediate or immediately
INA Initial approach
INBD Inbound
INC In cloud

INCERFA† Uncertainty phase
INFO† Information
INOP Inoperative
INP If not possible
INPR In progress
INS Inertial navigation system
INSTL Install or installed or installation
INSTR Instrument
INT Intersection
INTL International
INTRG Interrogator
INTRP Interrupt or interruption or interrupted
INTSF Intensify or intensifying
INTST Intensity
IR Ice on runway
IRS Inertial reference system
ISA International standard atmosphere
ISB Independent sideband
ISOL Isolated

J

JAN January
JTST Jet stream
JUL July
JUN June

K

KG Kilograms
KHZ Kilohertz
KIAS Knots indicated airspeed
KM Kilometres
KMH Kilometres per hour

KPA Kilopascal
KT Knots
KW Kilowatts

L

... L Left (preceded by runway designation number to identify a parallel runway)
L Locator (see LM, LO)
L Low pressure area or the centre of low pressure
LAM Logical acknowledgement (message type designator)
LAN Inland
LAT Latitude
LCA Local or locally or location or located
LDA Landing distance available
LDAH Landing distance available, helicopter
LDG Landing
LDI Landing direction indicator
LEN Length
LF Low frequency [30 to 300 kHz]
LGT Light or lighting
LGTD Lighted
LIH Light intensity high
LIL Light intensity low
LIM Light intensity medium
LINE Line (used in SIGMET)
LM Locator, middle
LMT Local mean time
LNAV† Lateral navigation
LNG Long (used to indicate the type of approach desired or required)
LO Locator, outer
LOC Localiser
LONG Longitude

LORAN† LORAN (long range air navigation system)

LOSS Airspeed or headwind loss

LPV Localiser performance with vertical guidance

LR The last message received by me was . . . (to be used in AFS as a procedure signal)

LRG Long range

LS The last message sent by me was . . . or Last message was . . . (to be used in AFS as a procedure signal)

LTD Limited

LTP Landing threshold point

LTT Landline teletypewriter

LV Light and variable (relating to wind)

LVE Leave or leaving

LVL Level

LVP Low visibility procedures

LYR Layer or layered

M

. . . M Metres (preceded by figures)

M . . . Mach number (followed by figures)

M . . . Minimum value of runway visual range (followed by figures in METAR/SPECI)

MAA Maximum authorised altitude

MAG Magnetic

MAHF Missed approach holding fix

MAINT Maintenance

MAP Aeronautical maps and charts

MAPT Missed approach point

MAR At sea

MAR March

MAS Manual Al simplex

MATF Missed approach turning fix

MAX Maximum

MAY May
MBST Microburst
MCA Minimum crossing altitude
MCW Modulated continuous wave
MDA Minimum descent altitude
MDF Medium frequency direction-finding station
MDH Minimum descent height
MEA Minimum en-route altitude
MEHT Minimum eye height over threshold (for visual approach slope indicator systems)
MET† Meteorological or meteorology
METAR† Aerodrome routine meteorological report (in meteorological code)
MET REPORT Local routine meteorological report (in abbreviated plain language)
MF Medium frequency [300 to 3 000 kHz]
MHDF Medium and high frequency direction finding stations (at the same location)
MHVDF Medium, high and very high frequency direction-finding stations (at the same location)
MHZ Megahertz
MID Mid-point (related to RVR)
MIFG Shallow fog
MIL Military
MIN* Minutes
MIS Missing . . . (transmission identification) (to be used in AFS as a procedure signal)
MKR Marker radio beacon
MLS‡ Microwave landing system
MM Middle marker
MNM Minimum
MNPS Minimum navigation performance specifications
MNT Monitor or monitoring or monitored
MNTN Maintain

MOA Military operating area

MOC Minimum obstacle clearance (required)

MOCA Minimum obstacle clearance altitude

MOD Moderate (used to indicate the intensity of weather phenomena, interference or static reports, e.g. MODRA = moderate rain)

MON Above mountains

MON Monday

MOPS† Minimum operational performance standards

MOV Move or moving or movement

MPS Metres per second

MRA Minimum reception altitude

MRG Medium range

MRP ATS/MET reporting point

MS Minus

MSA Minimum sector altitude

MSAS† Multifunctional transport satellite (MTSAT) satellite-based augmentation system

MSAW Minimum safe altitude warning

MSG Message

MSL Mean sea level

MSR# Message . . . (transmission identification) has been misrouted (to be used in AFS as a procedure signal)

MSSR Monopulse secondary surveillance radar

MT Mountain

MTU Metric units

MTW Mountain waves

MVDF Medium and very high frequency direction- finding stations (at the same location)

MWO Meteorological watch office

MX Mixed type of ice formation (white and clear)

N

N No distinct tendency (in RVR during previous 10 minutes)

N North or northern latitude

NADP Noise abatement departure procedure

NASC† National AIS system centre

NAT North Atlantic

NAV Navigation

NAVAID Navigational Aid

NB Northbound

NBFR Not Before

NC No change

NCD No cloud detected (used in automated METAR/SPECI)

NDB‡ Non-directional radio beacon

NDV No directional variations available (used in automated METAR/SPECI)

NE North-east

NEB North-eastbound

NEG No or negative or permission not granted or that is not correct

NGT Night

NIL*† None or I have nothing to send to you

NM Nautical miles

NML Normal

NN No name, unnamed

NNE North-north-east

NNW North-north-west

NO No (negative) (to be used in AFS as a procedure signal)

NOF International NOTAM office

NOSIG† No significant change (used in trend-type landing forecasts)

NOTAM† A notice distributed by means of telecommunication containing information concerning the establishment, condition or change in any aeronautical facility, service, procedure or hazard, the timely knowledge of which is essential to personnel concerned with flight operations

NOV November

NOZ‡ Normal operating zone
NPA Non-precision approach
NR Number
NRH No reply heard
NS Nimbostratus
NSC Nil significant cloud
NSE Navigation system error
NSW Nil significant weather
NTL National
NTZ‡ No transgression zone
NW North-west
NWB North-westbound
NXT Next

O

OAC Oceanic area control centre
OAS Obstacle assessment surface
OBS Observe or observed or observation
OBSC Obscure or obscured or obscuring
OBST Obstacle
OCA Obstacle clearance altitude
OCA Oceanic control area
OCC Occulting (light)
OCH Obstacle clearance height
OCNL Occasional or occasionally
OCS Obstacle clearance surface
OCT October
OFZ Obstacle free zone
OGN Originate (to be used in AFS as a procedure signal)
OHD Overhead
OIS Obstacle identification surface
OK* We agree or It is correct (to be used in AFS as a procedure signal)

OKTAS Unit used to express the extent of cloud cover, equal to one eighth of the sky.

OLDI† On-line data interchange

OM Outer marker

OPA Opaque, white type of ice formation

OPC Control indicated is operational control

OPMET† Operational meteorological (information)

OPN Open or opening or opened

OPR Operator or operate or operative or operating or operational

OPS† Operations

O/R On request

ORD Order

OSV Ocean station vessel

OTP On top

OTS Organised track system

OUBD Outbound

OVC Overcast

P

P . . . Maximum value of wind speed or runway visual range (followed by figures in METAR/SPECI and TAF)

P . . . Prohibited area (followed by identification)

PA Precision approach

PALS Precision approach lighting system (specify category)

PANS Procedures for air navigation services

PAPI† Precision approach path indicator

PAR‡ Precision approach radar

PARL Parallel

PATC . . . Precision approach terrain chart (followed by name/title)

PAX Passenger(s)

PBN Performance-based navigation

PCD Proceed or proceeding

PCL Pilot-controlled lighting

PCN Pavement classification number
PDC‡ Pre-departure clearance
PDG Procedure design gradient
PER Performance
PERM Permanent
PIB Pre-flight information bulletin
PJE Parachute jumping exercise
PL Ice pellets
PLA Practice low approach
PLN Flight plan
PLVL Present level
PN Prior notice required
PNR Point of no return
PO Dust/sand whirls (dust devils)
POB Persons on board
POSS Possible
PPI Plan position indicator
PPR Prior permission required
PPSN Present position
PRFG Aerodrome partially covered by fog
PRI Primary
PRKG Parking
PROB† Probability
PROC Procedure
PROV Provisional
PRP Point-in-space reference point
PS Plus
PSG Passing
PSN Position
PSP Pierced steel plank
PSR‡ Primary surveillance radar
PSYS Pressure system(s)
PTN Procedure turn
PTS Polar track structure

PWR Power

Q

QD Do you intend to ask me for a series of bearings? or I intend to ask you for a series of bearings (to be used in radiotelegraphy as a Q Code)

QDM‡ Magnetic heading (zero wind)

QDR Magnetic bearing

QFE‡ Atmospheric pressure at aerodrome elevation (or at runway threshold)

QFU Magnetic orientation of runway

QGE What is my distance to your station? or Your distance to my station is (distance figures and units) (to be used in radiotelegraphy as a Q Code)

QJH Shall I run my test tape/a test sentence? or Run your test tape/a test sentence (to be used in AFS as a Q Code)

QNH‡ Altimeter sub-scale setting to obtain elevation when on the ground

QSP Will you relay to . . . free of charge? or I will relay to . . . free of charge (to be used in AFS as a Q Code)

QTA Shall I cancel telegram number . . .? or Cancel telegram number . . . (to be used in AFS as a Q Code)

QTE True bearing

QTF Will you give me the position of my station according to the bearings taken by the D/F stations which you control? or The position of your station according to the bearings taken by the D/F stations that I control was . . . latitude . . . longitude (or other indication of position), class . . . at . . . hours (to be used in radiotelegraphy as a Q Code)

QUAD Quadrant

QUJ Will you indicate the TRUE track to reach you? or The TRUE track to reach me is . . . degrees at . . . hours (to be used in radiotelegraphy as a Q Code)

R

... R Right (preceded by runway designation number to identify a parallel runway)

R Rate of turn

R Red

R ... Restricted area (followed by identification)

R ... Runway (followed by figures in METAR/SPECI)

R* Received (acknowledgement of receipt) (to be used in AFS as a procedure signal)

RA Rain

RA Resolution advisory

RAC Rules of the air and air traffic services

RAG Ragged

RAG Runway arresting gear

RAI Runway alignment indicator

RAIM† Receiver autonomous integrity monitoring

RASC† Regional AIS system centre

RASS Remote altimeter setting source

RB Rescue boat

RCA Reach cruising altitude

RCC Rescue coordination centre

RCF Radio-communication failure (message type designator)

RCH Reach or reaching

RCL Runway centre line

RCLL Runway centre line light(s)

RCLR Re-cleared

RCP‡ Required communication performance

RDH Reference datum height

RDL Radial

RDO Radio

RE Recent (used to qualify weather phenomena, e.g. RERA = recent rain)

REC Receive or receiver

REDL Runway edge light(s)

REF Reference to . . . or refer to . . .

REG Registration

RENL Runway end light(s)

REP Report or reporting or reporting point

REQ Request or requested

RERTE Re-route

RESA Runway end safety area

RF Constant radius arc to a fix

RG Range (lights)

RHC Right-hand circuit

RIF Re-clearance in flight

RIME† Rime (used in aerodrome warnings)

RITE Right (direction of turn)

RL Report leaving

RLA Relay to

RLCE Request level change en route

RLLS Runway lead-in lighting system

RLNA Request level not available

RMK Remark

RNAV† Area navigation

RNG Radio range

RNP‡ Required navigation performance

ROBEX† Regional OPMET bulletin exchange (scheme)

ROC Rate of climb

ROD Rate of descent

RON Receiving only

RPDS Reference path data selector

RPI‡ Radar position indicator

RPL Repetitive flight plan

RPLC Replace or replaced

RPS Radar position symbol

RPT* Repeat or I repeat (to be used in AFS as a procedure signal)

RQ* Request (to be used in AFS as a procedure signal)

RQMNTS Requirements

RQP Request flight plan (message type designator)

RQS Request supplementary flight plan (message type designator)

RR Report reaching

RRA (or RRB, RRC . . . etc., in sequence) Delayed meteorological message (message type designator)

RSC Rescue sub-centre

RSCD Runway surface condition

RSP Responder beacon

RSR En-route surveillance radar

RSS Root sum square

RTD Delayed (used to indicate delayed meteorological message; message type designator)

RTE Route

RTF Radiotelephone

RTG Radiotelegraph

RTHL Runway threshold light(s)

RTN Return or returned or returning

RTODAH Rejected take-off distance available, helicopter

RTS Return to service

RTT Radio-teletypewriter

RTZL Runway touchdown zone light(s)

RUT Standard regional route transmitting frequencies

RV Rescue vessel

RVR‡ Runway visual range

RVSM‡ Reduced vertical separation minimum (300 m (1 000 ft)) between FL 290 and FL 410

RWY Runway

S

S South or southern latitude

S . . . State of the sea (followed by figures in METAR/SPECI)

SA Sand

SALS Simple approach lighting system

SAN Sanitary

SAP As soon as possible

SAR Search and rescue

SARPS Standards and Recommended Practices [ICAO]

SAT Saturday

SATCOM† Satellite communication

SB Southbound

SBAS† Satellite-based augmentation system

SC Stratocumulus

SCT Scattered

SD Standard deviation

SDBY Stand by

SDF Step down fix

SE South-east

SEA Sea (used in connection with sea-surface temperature and state of the sea)

SEB South-eastbound

SEC Seconds

SECN Section

SECT Sector

SELCAL† Selective calling system

SEP September

SER Service or servicing or served

SEV Severe (used e.g. to qualify icing and turbulence reports)

SFC Surface

SG Snow grains

SGL Signal

SH . . . Shower (followed by RA = rain, SN = snow, PL = ice pellets, GR = hail, GS = small hail and/or snow pellets or combinations thereof, e.g. SHRASN = showers of rain and snow)

SHF Super high frequency [3 000 to 30 000 MHz]

SI International system of units

SID† Standard instrument departure

SIF Selective identification feature

SIG Significant

SIGMET† Information concerning en-route weather phenomena which may affect the safety of aircraft operations

SIMUL Simultaneous or simultaneously

SIWL Single isolated wheel load

SKED Schedule or scheduled

SLP Speed limiting point

SLW Slow

SMC Surface movement control

SMR Surface movement radar

SN Snow

SNOCLO Aerodrome closed due to snow (used in METAR/SPECI)

SNOWTAM† Special series NOTAM notifying the presence or removal of hazardous conditions due to snow, ice, slush or standing water associated with snow, slush and ice on the movement area, by means of a specific format

SOC Start of climb

SPECI† Aerodrome special meteorological report (in meteorological code)

SPECIAL† Local special meteorological report (in abbreviated plain language)

SPI Special position indicator

SPL Supplementary flight plan (message type designator)

SPOC SAR point of contact

SPOT† Spot wind

SQ Squall

SQL Squall line

SR Sunrise

SRA Surveillance radar approach

SRE Surveillance radar element of precision approach radar system

SRG Short range
SRR Search and rescue region
SRY Secondary
SS Sandstorm
SS Sunset
SSB Single sideband
SSE South-south-east
SSR‡ Secondary surveillance radar
SST Supersonic transport
SSW South-south-west
ST Stratus
STA Straight-in approach
STAR† Standard instrument arrival
STD Standard
STF Stratiform
STN Station
STNR Stationary
STOL Short take-off and landing
STS Status
STWL Stop-way light(s)
SUBJ Subject to
SUN Sunday
SUP Supplement (AIP Supplement)
SUPPS Regional supplementary procedures
SVC Service message
SVCBL Serviceable
SW South-west
SWB South-westbound
SWY Stopway

T

T Temperature
... T True (preceded by a bearing to indicate reference to True

North)
TA Traffic advisory
TA Transition altitude
TAA Terminal arrival altitude
TACAN† UHF tactical air navigation aid
TAF† Aerodrome forecast (in meteorological code)
TA/H Turn at an altitude/height
TAIL† Tail wind
TAR Terminal area surveillance radar
TAS True airspeed
TAX Taxiing or taxi
TC Tropical cyclone
TCAC Tropical cyclone advisory centre
TCAS RA† Traffic alert and collision avoidance system resolution
advisory
TCH Threshold crossing height
TCU Towering cumulus
TDO Tornado
TDZ Touchdown zone
TECR Technical reason
TEL Telephone
TEMPO† Temporary or temporarily
TF Track to fix
TFC Traffic
TGL Touch-and-go landing
TGS Taxiing guidance system
THR Threshold
THRU Through
THU Thursday
TIBA† Traffic information broadcast by aircraft
TIL† Until
TIP Until past . . . (place)
TKOF Take-off

TL ... Till (followed by time by which weather change is forecast to end)

TLOF Touchdown and lift-off area

TMA‡ Terminal control area

TN ... Minimum temperature (followed by figures in TAF)

TNA Turn altitude

TNH Turn height

TO ... To ... (place)

TOC Top of climb

TODA Take-off distance available

TODAH Take-off distance available, helicopter

TOP† Cloud top

TORA Take-off run available

TOX Toxic

TP Turning point

TR Track

TRA Temporary reserved airspace

TRANS Transmits or transmitter

TREND† Trend forecast

TRL Transition level

TROP Tropopause

TS Thunderstorm (in aerodrome reports and forecasts, TS used alone means thunder heard but no precipitation at the aerodrome)

TS ... Thunderstorm (followed by RA = rain, SN = snow, PL = ice pellets, GR = hail, GS = small hail and/or snow pellets or combinations thereof, e.g. TSRASN = thunderstorm with rain and snow)

TSUNAMI† Tsunami (used in aerodrome warnings)

TT Teletypewriter

TUE Tuesday

TURB Turbulence

T-VASIS† T visual approach slope indicator system

TVOR Terminal VOR

TWR Aerodrome control tower or aerodrome control

TWY Taxiway
TWYL Taxiway-link
TX ... Maximum temperature (followed by figures in TAF)
TXT* Text (when the abbreviation is used to request a repetition, the question mark (IMI) precedes the abbreviation, e.g. IMI TXT) (to be used in AFS as a procedure signal)
TYP Type of aircraft
TYPH Typhoon

U

U Upward (tendency in RVR during previous 10 minutes)
UA Unmanned aircraft
UAB ... Until advised by ...
UAC Upper area control centre
UAR Upper air route
UAS Unmanned aircraft system
UDF Ultra high frequency direction-finding station
UFN Until further notice
UHDT Unable higher due traffic
UHF‡ Ultra high frequency [300 to 3 000 MHz]
UIC Upper information centre
UIR‡ Upper flight information region
ULR Ultra long range
UNA Unable
UNAP Unable to approve
UNL Unlimited
UNREL Unreliable
UP Unidentified precipitation (used in automated METAR/SPECI)
U/S Unserviceable
UTA Upper control area
UTC‡ Coordinated Universal Time

V

... V ... Variations from the mean wind direction
(preceded and followed by figures in METAR/SPECI, e.g.
350V070)
VA Heading to an altitude
VA Volcanic ash
VAAC Volcanic ash advisory centre
VAC ... Visual approach chart (followed by name/title)
VAL In valleys
VAN Runway control van
VAR Magnetic variation
VAR Visual-aural radio range
VASIS Visual approach slope indicator systems
VC ... Vicinity of the aerodrome (followed by FG = fog, FC = funnel
cloud, SH = shower, PO = dust/sand whirls, BLDU = blowing dust,
BLSA = blowing sand, BLSN = blowing snow, DS = dust-storm, SS =
sandstorm, TS = thunderstorm or VA = volcanic ash, e.g. VCFG =
vicinity fog)
VCY Vicinity
VDF Very high frequency direction-finding station
VER Vertical
VFR‡ Visual flight rules
VHF‡ Very high frequency [30 to 300 MHz]
VI Heading to an intercept
VIP‡ Very important person
VIS Visibility
VLF Very low frequency [3 to 30 kHz]
VLR Very long range
VM Heading to a manual termination
VMC‡ Visual meteorological conditions
VNAV† Vertical navigation
VOLMET† Meteorological information for aircraft in flight
VOR‡ VHF omnidirectional radio range
VORTAC† VOR and TACAN combination
VOT VOR airborne equipment test facility

VPA Vertical path angle
VPT Visual manoeuvre with prescribed track
VRB Variable
VSA By visual reference to the ground
VSP Vertical speed
VTF Vector to final
VTOL Vertical take-off and landing
VV . . . Vertical visibility (followed by figures in METAR/SPECI and TAF)

W

W West or western longitude
W White
W . . . Sea-surface temperature (followed by figures in METAR/SPECI)
WAAS† Wide area augmentation system
WAC. . . World Aeronautical Chart — ICAO 1:1 000 000 (followed by name/title)
WAFC World area forecast centre
WB Westbound
WBAR Wing bar lights
WDI Wind direction indicator
WDSPR Widespread
WED Wednesday
WEF With effect from or effective from
WGS-84 World Geodetic System — 1984
WI Within
WID Width or wide
WIE With immediate effect or effective immediately
WILCO† Will comply
WIND Wind
WIP Work in progress
WKN Weaken or weakening

WNW West-north-west
WO Without
WPT Way-point
WRNG Warning
WS Wind shear
WSPD Wind speed
WSW West-south-west
WT Weight
WTSPT Waterspout
WWW Worldwide web
WX Weather

X

X Cross
XBAR Crossbar (of approach lighting system)
XNG Crossing
XS Atmospherics

Y

Y Yellow
YCZ Yellow caution zone (runway lighting)
YES* Yes (affirmative) (to be used in AFS as a procedure signal)
YR Your

Z

Z Coordinated Universal Time (in meteorological messages)

----

† When radiotelephony is used, the abbreviations and terms are
transmitted as spoken words.
‡ When radiotelephony is used, the abbreviations and terms are
transmitted using the individual letters in non-phonetic form.

* Signal is also available for use in communicating with stations of the maritime mobile service.

Signal for use in the teletypewriter service only.

ACKNOWLEDGMENTS

I wish to thank a few people who helped my flying career, whether they realise it or not, our fun conversations or the serious chats we had and the discussions around flying, made this book possible.

As I worked through the list of everyone who has influenced my aviation career, it is incredible to see the number of people I will always be grateful to. Thank you.

Neville Swan (first gliding instructor)
Craig McNeal (first power flying instructor)
Aaron Shipman
Aaron 'AJ' Jeffery
Aaron Pearce
Aaron Marshall
Adam Eltham
Aiden Campbell
Alan Beck QSM
Alistair Blake
Amiria Wallis

Anastasios Raptis
Andrew Gormlie
Andrew Hope
Andrew Lorimer
Andrew Love
Andrew Sunde
Andrew Telfer
Andy Mackay
Andy Stevenson MNZM
Angelo Cruz
Ben Lee
Ben Marcus
Ben Pryor NZGM
Benjamin James
Bevan Dewes
Bill Reid
Bradley Marsh
Brett Emeny
Brett Nicholls
Bruce Lynch
Bryn Lockie
Carlo Santoro
Carlton Campbell
Chantel Strooh
Charles J. Cook
Chris Barry
Chris Bromley
Chris Pond
Chris Satler
Chris Sperou OAM
Christina Harvey
Christoph Berthoud
Conor Neill
Cosmo Mead

Craig Piner
Craig Rook
Craig Speck
Craig Steel
Craig Walecki
Damien Campbell
Daniel Campbell
Darren Crabb
Daryl Gillett
Dave Blackwell
David Brown
Dave Campbell
Dave Cogan
Dave Hayman
Dave Rouse
David Lowy AM
David Morgan
David Saunders
David Wilkinson
Dennis Eckhoff
Derry Belcher
Desmond Barry
Don Lockie
Donovan Burns
Doug Batten
Doug Brown
Doug Burrell
Dwight Weston
Enya Mae McPherson
Eric Morgan
Eva Keim
Flo Smith
Frank Parker
Gareth Wheeler

Gavin Conroy
Gavin Trethewey
Gavin Weir
Gene De Marco
Geoff Cooper
George Oldfield JP
Giovanni Nustrini
Graeme 'Spud' Spurdle
Graham Lake
Graham Nevill
Graham Orphan
Grant Armishaw
Grant 'Muddy' Murdoch
Greg Quinn
Guy Bourke
Harvey Lockie
Hayden Leech
HH Prince Faisal bin Abdulla bin Mohammed Saud
Ian Lilley
Ian 'Iggy' Wood
Imogen Ling
James Aldridge
Jamie Wagner
Jason Alexander
Jason Haggitt DSD
Jay McIntyre
Jed Melling
Jill McCaw
Jim Rankin DSD
Jock MacLachlan
Joe Oldfield
John Duxfield ARCOM
John Gemmell
John Lamont

John Martin
John McCaw
Jonathan Bowen
Joseph D'Ath
Josh Camp
Juan Ferandoes
Jurgis Kairys
Karl Stol
Keith McKenzie QSM
Keith Skilling
Keith Stephens
Kenny Love
Kermit Weeks
Kevin Langley
Kevin Vile
Kirsty Coleman
Kishan Bhashyam
Kris Vette
Lawrence Acket
Liberio Riosa
Lionel Page
Liz King (Mother Goose)
Lloyd Galloway
Loïc Ifrah
Louisa 'Choppy' Patterson
Malcolm Clement
Martin Schulze
Mark Helliwell
Mark Lowndes
Mary Patterson
Matt Hall
Matt Ledger
Maurizio Folini
Melissa Andrzejewski (nee Pemberton)

Michael Bach
Michael Jeffs
Mike Clark
Mike Foster
Mike Harvey
Mike Jorgenson
Mike Read
Mike Slack
Nando Parrado
Nathan Graves
Nick Cree
Nick Tarascio
Nigel Cooper
Nigel Lamb
Nina Hayman
Paul Andronicou
Paul 'Huggy' Hughan
Paul 'Simmo' Simmons AM CSM
Pete Meadows
Pete Pring Shambler
Peter Harper
Peter Jefferies
Peter Thorpe
Phil Freeman
Phill Hooker
Pip Borrman
Ray Burns
Ray Richards
Reuben Muir
Rex Pemberton
Richard Button
Richard Hectors
Richard Hood
Rev. Dr Richard Waugh QSM

Richie McCaw ONZ
Rick Watson
Rob Fox
Rob Fry
Rob Mackley
Rob Neil
Rob Owens
Rob Weavers
Robert Burns
Roy Crane
Roy Cunningham
Ruan Heynike
Ruth Nisbet
Ryan Brooks
Ryan Francis
Sam Elimelech
Scott 'Macka' McKenzie
Sean Perrett
Shaun Clark
Shaun Roseveare
Simon J Gault
Simon Lockie
Simon Mundell
Simone Moro
SQNLDR Les Munro CNZM DSO QSO DFC JP
Steve Ahrens
Steve Wallace
Stephen Boyce
Stephen Death
Steve Gibson
Steve Newland
Steve Jurd
Steven Perreau
Stu Wards

Tasos Raptis
Tee Jay Sullivan
Tim Marshall
Sir Tim Wallis
Todd O'Hara
Tracy Dixon
Wayne Fowler
Wayne Ormrod
Wayne Thompson
Vaughan Davis
Yoshihide 'Yoshi' Muroya

AVGAS COFFEE

Fuel the need for speed and fly high with **Avgas Coffee**

We love the smell of avgas in the morning, so we combined our two passions – coffee and aviation. Our team has 50 years of experience in roasting and blending, and our master roaster ensures optimum flavours are extracted from the beans during every stage of the process. **Avgas Coffee's** three blends – *Maverick, Skyhawk* and *Blackhawk* are HaCCP, ISO9001, and Halal certified. We also have Freeze Dried *Macchi* and *Eagle EX* capsules.

With our subscription offer, you can save up to another 20%*, ensuring you never run out of **Avgas Coffee**.

Go to www.avgas.coffee, enter your name and email, and spin the wheel for a chance to **win*** up to 30% off your online order.

Blue skies!

*New Zealand and Australia only

ABOUT THE AUTHOR

With a passion for aviation passed on from his father who worked in the National Airways Corporation (NAC) office in Auckland, New Zealand. Fletcher often heard about the NAC DC3 Kaimai Ranges crash, this had made an impact on his father as he knew one of the flight attendants killed in the accident.

As a teenager, Fletcher knew the youngest instructor on his first gliding course who was sadly killed in a glider crash some months after that course.

Over his flying carrier, and during his adventures filming extreme aviators around the world, the deeper Fletcher read into understanding the situations pilots got into, and the more he understood the factors might lead to poor decision making in the skies above.

Coupled with twenty years of experience working with global entrepreneurs through EO (Entrepreneurs Organisation), training them to experience share between each other and to learn from any mistakes, Fletcher selected and compiled these stories to help us learn from others. To ensure current and future pilots will be safe in the skies.

www.fletchermckenzie.com

Printed in Great Britain
by Amazon